# Winners Circle of Dreams

No matter how many times you fall down in your life it matters how you rise up and get back up again you are the winner.

By C. Walden © 2012.

All rights reserved.

No part of this book may be reproduced of transmitted in any manner what so ever without written permission, except in the case of brief quotations embodied in critic articles and reviews

For more information
Contact winnerscircleofdreams@gmail.com
cdwalden@hotmail.com

## Dedication

This book is dedicated to those all around the world, who dare to dream, action their dreams to make it happen.

To my parents Hilda & Ray .thank you for the kind words **"that life is one big journey",** full of surprises, you gave me the wisdom to always believe you can do anything and have the courage and fight, you never know what tomorrow will bring, all is possible if you work hard, don't quit and never give up on your dreams

Thank you lord that you blessed me with a beautiful wife of 26 years, Angela I love you so much, you have been my rock and firm foundation and, inspiration amongst the good seasons and the bad.

Our 4 children Alisha, Jeremy, Andrew, Jessie, how special & unique you are, I love you all, dreams they do come true, it's all about how much you want them.

To my Brothers, Sisters, Extended family, mother and farther in-law, personal friends, who believed in my dream, thank you for your sincere love and compassion as I walked to the start line, completed my outstanding journey, finished the race that lead me, to where I am today, my love goes with you all , International Author & Keynote Speaker **CD Walden**

# The Quest

In late November 2011, My wife and I were living in a tiny 1 bed room cottage, with, 1 cat and my teenage daughter sleeping on the floor, sick, depressed, just over broke, little did I know that the environment I was in, would change my life dramatically, I would find out who I could become, to propel me from ordinary to extraordinary.

From turning up at the starting line and going through the trials of overcoming challenges and obstacles, a thought, change in mind-set, determination, commitment, vision, big dream, action, to reality, I completed the journey and finished the race, Thus the book Winners Circle of Dreams was created & born, and now an International Self Published Author.

We all can talk the talk, hear about success, but do we action our walk to success, and how much we want it.

What is your success? Are we prepared to pay the price? Stepping out and away from our comfort zone of failure, too challenge ourselves, if you have a big dream and you are searching for success that you desire or maybe it's time for you to make that change I honestly and truly believe from my heart it is highly recommend you, Family, Friends, Teenagers, Young Adults, Adults, read Winners Circle of Dreams today.

 It's not about the cover and name of the book, it's the winning ingredients inside the cover, that will inspire you to advance forward from where you are now.

 Many times we have been winners in our everyday lives, just think about the many blessing you have had, you can count them on your fingers more than the defeats you will ever have in your life time, be grateful you do have the gift and the power to win

Would you like to know how I mastered and engineered my own success to become an author? "Read on", tip no 1, I become like a thick skinned rhino, nothing <u>like procrastination & adversity</u> was going to detour, derail, hold me back or stop me from doing the unthinkable in life. There is the only way to find our own success, and that starts with you.

# Table of contents

## Chapter 1
- Dream big.
- It's free to dream.
- Kids love to dream.
- Dreams can help your teenagers.

## Chapter 2
- Adults need to dare to dream again like kids.
- Christmas Dreams.
- The Birthday wish.
- Put yourself on the Big Dreamers List.

## Chapter 3
- The dentist who excited me with dreams.
- Dreams are opportunities waiting to evolve.
- You know it's never too late.
- I was dreaming of Xfactor 2013.

## Chapter 4
- We are born to win.
- Wishing and hoping.
- Dreaming and Doing.
- Without Direction, it won't happen.
- Time for change how about you.

# Chapter 5

- Write down your dreams today, you can see your future.
- Voyager of the seas dream cruise, taking a photo just doesn't cut.
- 3% v.i.p club of success.
- 97% holiday club ticket to someday.
- Look there's a price to pay to dream.

# Chapter 6

- Have you worked out, what your top dream is yet.
- Visualize your dreams use affirmation.
- You have to keep Dreaming to stay in the game long enough to win.
- Try P.P.P so powerful it works every time.
- Why successful dreamers do, what they do, never quit.
- Guard your dream, mind, body and heart.
- My immune system protects me, how about you.
- Wear protective clothing 24/7.
- Diamonds in the rough, incredible still they shine.
- Guard your dream, mind, body and heart at all times
- Share your big dreams with the butterfly not with the spiders.

# Chapter 7

- Excuses, Excuses, Excuses Start winning today.
- Obstacle v obligation = opportunity.
- I did whatever it takes to get to the grand finale.
- I will Enjoy Today I will Plan for Tomorrow.
- Unlimited dreams and potential inside of you.

## Chapter 8
- No worries, people will think you're crazy.
- The journey commit, it's worth it.
- Let courage lead you closer to your dream.
- Don't let your past hold you back.
- Need advice you need a coach.
- Time waits for no one, not even dreamers.
- Time and momentum.

## Chapter 9
- Its easy focus on the outcome, start winning first to give yourself a chance.
- You must start with a process and performance plan today, to see the outcome.
- It's never too late to pick up on your scattered dream.
- How to become a conqueror of fear and negativity.
- Your Dreams don't have to be complicated.
- If I can do it, you can to, Imagine the possibilities.

## Chapter 10
Power Dream Principles
- 3 Ds.
- 3 Rs
- 3 Es
- 3 As
- 3 Ms

# Introduction

Who ever thought I would try to write a book called Winners Circle of Dreams, try be a successful author, and try my hand at being be a motivational speaker, I am just as excited as you are, and are mindful that I don't have all the answers to life, in my book, but if it can be of any benefit towards you filling your mindset with positive inspiration and action ,fast tracking you to move forward in your life, then this book is doing its job, reaching out and touching the hearts of many people around the world,  I am so grateful, that you will spend the time, and read the book winners circle of dreams, I know there are so many great tips that will help you discover the, what's, who's, where, why, how, in your life.

After all, this entire book is designed to be, very simple, not complicated and very user friendly to read and use.

The book Winners circle of dreams will help enlighten, encourage you to dream and win for you.

Well it has taken me 52 years to navigate, have the courage, and the passion and desire and plan to pursue, take a journey and head in the right direction and start living the winners circle of dreams, so dust off the cobwebs, get rid of skeletons of the past, don't slide backward, go forward, get excited, soar with the eagles.

I have always been a dreamer, which started from when I was a child, and for most of my life, and it's that dreaming that's given me a burning desire never to give up.

I know we all as human beings are looking for that passion to dream and turn them into reality; it is achievable and so possible.

## 99% of you will fall in love with

## the book the other 1% percent I leave too the

**critic**, you see, I can't please everybody, and I wouldn't want to try, I know that everything in life is about learning, we still learn new things every day even at 52, we all should, I don't want to teach you about anything new, but just to remind you, on what you already know.

You see our dreams become possible
**1 When we confront time**
**2 We challenge ourselves**
**3 We master the highs and lows in our everyday lives to be the best we can be.**

And to tell you the truth there have been many great times, sad times and challenges in my life, this is what makes me the person I am today.

So read and enjoy and relax, you may like to make a change today, don't wait, dream about exciting possibilities waiting in front of you.

<u>**A winner's mentality fuelled by action**</u>: "Great dreams & stories happen to those, in the world, who can tell them." --**Ira Glass**


No matter how many times you fall down in your life, it matters how you rise up and get back up again you are the winner.

# Chapter 1

# Dream big

**Dream big, dream big, dream big, don't stop and you will win**

IVE always love the American dream and what it stands for, **Dream big & Nike just do it, go together** well, its time you did, and you owe it to yourself to dream big. Big dreamers are the ones who learn and earn and get big results. Small mined dreamers get small results and give up.
Dream big, nothing is impossible but possible and you will be successful
Most people cannot see themselves dreaming the big dream, in fact, ever having a dream. They are fearful and scared to take a risk and chance anything in life,

"So many people in their lifetime tend to put themselves down and class themselves as $2^{nd}$ class citizens with a second class attitude and performance in life". – **C.D Walden**

if you could just sit down, change your attitude, think about where your big dream can take you, and if you made a commitment today to dream big, you will be successful, you see most people need to visualize and picture themselves in the **house of their dreams**.

How about starting with a big dream, make it exciting e.g. writing a novel, how about a new car, or maybe losing weight , new house, better relationship, going to the most exotic places on a cruise ship,

# Dream big

around the world on holiday). Picture taking your wife shopping ,the motto is happy wife ,happy life ,happy kids , you both go shopping at a place like Harrods in London England , might seem crazy to think about shopping at the best stores and you got the

Money, because you turned your big dream into reality and the wife is all smiles.

You see the formula to making your big dream happen is.

**"To start with a big dream, find out what it is you love doing, and make gains and wins happen, have a reason, desire purpose to believe for you and your family".**

Success will come, the harder you work, and the luckier you will reap the benefits of the big dream.
The success that you want to become is by allowing yourself to dream big, is to get you out of your comfort zone, be like a thick skinned rhino nothing's going to hold me back or stop me from doing the unthinkable.

People who dream big, know who they are, what they are all about, and know which direction they are heading in life, they get better results than people who dream little, or don't even allow themselves to dream. It's so sad that some people really don't think it's worth it to imagine and think about a happier life for them.
**Dreaming big and believing big, plays an important role towards attainment of success.** You ever played any sport, part of winning the game is being willing to work as a team and to be prepared physically and mentally, to make the finals of any sport, just take a look at the American NFL finals of the Super Bowl there can only be two spots to make that big dream of playing in a super bowl final a reality. For people, sports people, top companies who dare to dream that are willing to work hard and pay a price; success can become a major reality.
All of us as parents have been in situations where we have had to scrape the barrel, just to get by from day to day , , heard that saying ,we keep doing what we keep doing ,keep getting what we keep getting , that's called insanity ,our lives will be the same if we

# Dream big

Don't have a dream.
We all think of lotto and think about the changes we all could have, I agree, I have bought a ticket without financial return, at least my big dream is for free and I have it within my heart and it's still burning inside I would love to be able to have those things that we all want, whether they are cars and boats or vacations,

**"I still think you can achieve your goals! Why by having a big dream and taking action".**

think: about the possibilities of a big dream, that can influence and change you for the rest of your life ,do it, if you put the hard work in , this is a life that only successful people dream of which offers independence, victory, financial freedom and the ability to make your own goals and decisions, and all that you want, both materially and in terms of your time, and freedom to do what you want!, when you want
I know of family friends solo mums solo dads granddads who have been trapped in the life of despair ,tiny dreams, poverty, coupon clipping ,second hand hand-outs . This could be you? Believe me, for a large majority of people this is all we can visualize, myself and family know what it's like on the so call bread line. Open your mind, your imagination, & your drive for success. Dream big today and make those dreams happen.

**"Get out of the rut and strut your way into living a good life".
CD Walden**


If you have a big dream, set a goal, then you are 1 of the special elite persons that has taken control and made a commitment to heading towards a better life .if you haven't got a big dream and are just wishing, then you are probably working for someone who is setting those goals for you. Dream big today and take action, don't stop and you will win.

# Dream big

Questions you may ask yourself.

**1** Am I happy?
**2** Do I want to change in my life?
**3** Is living the big dream lifestyle for me?


Here are 6 keynote winners of circle dreams tips to help you dream big.
**1** Do you want to dream big or small?
**2** Make a change, visualize your future
**3** Big dreams comes from within, but you need to write them down
**4** Take control of you big dream and own it
**5** Breathe, live, action your big dream.
**6** Get excited; have fun on your journey.

<u>**A winner's mentality fuelled by action**</u>: "There's always room for a big dream in one's life, and a story that can transport people to another place." --**J.K. Rowling**


No matter how many times you fall down in your life it matters how you rise up and get back up again you are the winner.

# It's free to dream.

**It's free to dream the dream**

Do you remember the kind of free dreams you had when you were young, or are you are still dreaming your life away.

## "Dreams can come to you in all forms of thought shape and size".

They can all be about fantasy, creative, horror, romance; adventure, death, fiction, and non-fiction leadership champions anything you desire as a thought

Think about it we all love to dream, we can daydream, like my wife, you could dream about the graduation day, there is no right or wrong to become a member of the winners circle of dreams club. Dreams have no limits in thought and untapped boundaries, human beings throughout history have been dreaming of images, ideas, emotions, and sensations occurring involuntarily in the mind during certain stages of sleep and in their conscious and when they relax.

Day dreaming, is a wondering mind full of intriguing events that have an effect on one who is thinking about the past present and future

Dreams can be a state of one imagination; in a trance for a split second .and can give you some sort of belief and hope and some sort of fantasy. Your dream can drive you to be passionate and fill your heart with heart's desire and excel you to achieve ones aspiration:

We all can dream of being a champion, hero, an influential leader and becoming a sports person and writer, a singer, having more money in the bank, teacher, and owning your own business, and dreaming about being the best you can be and want to be, or live the dream that is exceptionally gratifying, excellent, or beautiful: or fuelled sadness or victory

# Its free to dream

We dream of the new house and what it looks like , and how my new car runs like a dream .I experience a dream in my sleep and dreamed about x factor . Spending quality time to yourself, I find it very relaxing and it gives me a sense of being at peace with myself, you should too, and you can release the pressure off our everyday modern and demanding lifestyle we have today.

**"Our creator of the universe, in our life time has given to all of us, precious gifts".**

**Time**

**Choices**

**Free agency**

If you follow the powerful keynotes inserts and examples in the book winners circle of dreams, they will help your big dreams unfold and become a reality, you become the winner. .

Questions you may ask yourself

**1** It's free to dream, how do I get started?
**2** What would happen if my free dream became a reality?

6 Keynote winners circle of dreams tips it free to dream
**1** Start dreaming doesn't cost anything.
**2** Dreams about whatever
**3** Imagine the possibilities
**4** Where can I dream?
**5** I can dream & achieve anything.
**6** What dream and goal is important me right now


No matter how many times you fall down in your life it matters how you rise up and get back up again you are the winner.

# Kids love to dream.

"**Walt Disney**" once said "what would the world be like" if kids did not have a dream"
I know from past experience, as child myself; they were some of most wonderful and enjoyable years of my life, I wish I could turn back the clock. In today's society times have changed for parents ,who along with their kids are bomb barded with TV and internet IPods', apps, android ,blogging sites advertisings and considerable novelties of all sorts and to the dilemma of massive peer pressure ,that every kid is doing or having the same thing as the next child , or he or she's got that ,I want that too. I am a firm believer that great kids become wonderful kids when they know who they are, what direction they would like to pursue in life. Novelties in this day and age, there's so many to choose from you tend to get more frustrated picking the right one to choose. For my wife and I when I was working away from home, the toys and novelties didn't come into play that much, all the kids wanted was a good hug and say love you Dad.

As adults we want do the best for our kids, bringing up 4 kids as well, I could see the excitable dreams, which were going on in their lives also.

My kids were no exception to creative dreams , Looking at colourful scrap books and movies, like beauty and the beast, Cinderella, Donald duck to Mickey Mouse, Mr Magoo, Superman, Noddy, Star Wars, Harry Potter Santa coming to town or role play kids dress ups, kindergarten experiences & cooking or going to the shop, my children like all kids would imitate or mimic what they would see and hear, and guess what I found out as a parent, I had a great mind of my own, that at times, I just wanted revert back to be that dreamy kid again.

"All Kids are big dreamers; with a massive shopping list, they definitely know what they want".

# Kids love to dream

when it comes down to shopping, for the Christmas dream & wish list, birthday dream.

Research has stated one of the biggest dreams for most kids is go to Disneyland; it is the ultimate fantasy dream on the dream kid list.

Have you ever watched your kid's progress in their lives from day 1? From a baby, teething, crawling, walking. When they started kindergarten, through to primary school, you see the growth and changes, kids don't stay the same .kids must move on to pursue life, have you ever heard of a kid going back down a level, or going backward, another year because they didn't complete the educational level, it may be the case, I haven't heard of one personally, kids dreams are in much the same way, that they are taking in new experiences and new things in life, physically and mentally.

**"As parent be supportive and loving to your children, let them dream, equip them with the life's learning tools"**

I found out with my own, they are only kids for the short time, cherish moments of love.

Questions you may ask yourself.
**1** Am I helping my kids to dream?
**2** When was the last time I talk to my kids about their dreams?
**3** What did I dream about when I was a child?

Here are 6 keynote winner circles of dreams tips to help your kids dream
**1** Find out what it is your children love doing
**2** Encourage your children's gifts and talents
**3** Interact and Socialize with other children
**4** Don't live your dreams through your kids.
**5** Let you kid experiment new activities.
**6** Kids will pursue their own dreams and goals, support them, they need a shoulder to lean on.

# Every teenagers dream is inspired by different generations.

I wanted to write this special peace in my book and dedicate this insert to every teenager that will see and read this chapter.

> **"I would like to say, love your teenage kids, they are great, remember they have a place in history, and are the seeds for tomorrow's leaders, and next generation"**

Just as much as any other parent ,grandparents, solo mum ,solo dad, guardian, I have had 4 teenagers, Alisha ,Jeremy, Andrew who are now young adults who are our beautiful diamonds , we have one more teenager Jessie she is 15, to support and help right now, she is our beautiful diamond , later on as you continue reading this book ,there is a story about a diamond and its shining radiant light ,Angela and I love them all so much in their unique & special way . I can recall my days as a teenager so well, how I said, "if only I could turn back the clock", because they were good years for me.

**If you had a hard time in your teenage years, I do feel for you, I hope as you have travelled on in your journey that you have found what you have been looking for ,learnt a few lessons and taken a few hard knocks ,most of all learnt, how to forgive ,and love again .**

There are grandparent who grew up, that will Remember Bill Haley and the Comets, Elvis and his swinging hips of the 50's, The beetles of 64 and their love songs, such as "I want to hold your hand", they dreamed, conquered, inspired and influenced so many teenagers of their generations.

**Every generation has had its moment of glory; the 1970s was no exception,** the teens in my day were different than today's teens. I know, I ended up going to a country barn dance or community church hall and we all had a great time, you see I wasn't in a hurry to grow up as a teen, I know as teen I took responsibility for my actions, I respected my parents and girlfriends, I had a respect for the great outdoors and our beauty, I would also treat people & friends as whanau, and not my enemy.

# Every teenagers dream is inspired by different generations

Catching up on great times chilling out having FUN. Listening to groovy 70s music spinners ,Tavares, Commodores, Led zeppelin , the Who, Dragon, Elton John, hot summers, Hiking, biking, walking -camping - physical stuff, that did not cost a cent, **just a simple life, this is what made teens dream** ,we had no hang-ups, not like the pressures of today's teens. I remember going to town rocking up in my jeans We were not materialistic, nobody cared about what you looked like or how ugly you were ,worrying about the next best thing .Going to town was a treat to watch James bonds 007 live and let die at the pictures at the old Hamilton's regent theatre building , buying ice creams ,and chocolate smarty's listening to them roll down the aisle we just wanted to have fun, just like the teens of today we had to deal with teen issues too, like put up with the pimples , puppetry, zits ,nits, girls, boys ,college days, the sex talk with mum and dad , the first taste of alcohol, the first ciggie marijuana , run away from home, nobody loves me scenarios.

Questions you may ask yourself.
**1** Have I told my teen, what it was like back in my day, when I was a teen?
**2** Did I have teen skeletons in the closet; I'm not willing to share? Was I a 'goodie goodie 2 shoes' teenager back in my day?
**3** What did I dream about when I was a teenager?

Here are 5 keynote things I learnt as a teenager
**1** I Respect my parent
**2** Good friends were important
**3** Took the time to chill out and have fun
**4** Words of encouragement
**5** I always cared for other

## How to inspire your teen in today world
Teens today are now living in a different world than I did at their age. In today's environment the world is changing so fast, even for

# Every teenagers dream is inspired by different generations

us as parent and caregivers, life seems scary at times. Have you heard the saying no change lots of pain ,it is so important that we keep up with the pace of our youth and technology , but there's one thing that we do have as adults ,that we can bring to the table and that is, we have been around for a very long time ,with all advances in life there's still ,are choices that have to be made.

We should really encourage our teens "To dream and dream big, say too every teenager "the sky is the limit"

Don't stop dreaming ,this is where the power of belief come from within , As for a lot of teens out there ,they don't hear the word "dream" ever spoken in their lives and setting goals about ambition and success , you are only as good as what you have been handed down from your parents too your teen, if as a parent or guardian you have not talked about a dream to them, well how can they have hopes and dreams and master the abundance and accomplishments a dream with great future has to offer, for their wellbeing and future , we must spend time to communicate with our teenagers and listen to what they have to say. I know with my own children I listened to what they had to say, my daughter Alisha wanted to go to university, and study fine arts and I said to her, you can become a doctor at otago university and you get paid great money, but no she wanted to study in Auckland, I realise now that if she didn't follow her dream and passion she would have been unhappy.

We as parent are so happy with her choice, we used our wisdom and judgement to help her decide, she is on the way to attaining her degree

If you're Teenager has a passion for a dream

**"Let them define their own goals and dreams, it is better that they get excited about something they are so hungry about and have the drive and the reason and belief"**

There is that saying, "you can lead a horse to water", but you can't make them drink, as my dad said this is what life is all about. ,

# Every teenagers dream is inspired by different generations

Sometimes we hate things we have to do, like earning money, so we can put food on the table, it's not our dream job, but we learn and live another tomorrow. I know with my two teenagers sons I was hoping that they would become great NZ All blacks I lived and breathed rugby for me, and

**"I thought I was helping the boys, it was my passion I was putting on to the boys and they felt that pressure"**

As a dad I'm glad the two boys have pursued their own dreams and aspirations and if in any way "boys" you felt uncomfortable, "I say sorry"

Too many parents passion tend be extended on to the life of their teens in their dreams and are landed with the high expectations of something that has been put on them.

**"We as parents have to turn this around and work with our teenagers collectively"**

Be their best friend, love them, not become a enemy, and let them make a decision about their own lives, so they feel inspired and not bottled up like a fly trapped in jam jar, or worse, trapped in a spider web. Read the chapter about spiders later on in the book. We can support our teens by giving ideas and put life tools on the collective table, help with a blue print vision of how they see their future, providing them with information in the way of education, and careers.

Angela and I talk to a family friend Mr B Schroder who always came around to our house; he would always have a chat with our children, and ask them, that same question, time and time again, what do you want to be someday? He sold for a company called Rewleighs, he told us about the realities of sales, when he first started. He told us, there is a starting point for every dream and anything you do in life, you see it's all about hard work and passion, a sales man like me will call 10 people today and get one sale, and tomorrow I will see ten people today and get 2 sales

# Every teenagers dream is inspired by different generations

## "I realized I was getting better and better at what I was good at today than yesterday I was winning".

The more teen-agers accept responsibility, for themselves, the more they will stay control of their destiny and lives, the more confident they will become. Deciding what they want and working to achieve it, is a key component to being a responsible person. A thing call learning, experience, value

Help your teenager, if you let them find and pick out their reason, why, how and where they are heading. Today and tomorrow it can only get better.

Questions you may ask yourself
**1** How many times do I have a good conversation with my teen?
**2** Do I spend more time doing things together with my teen, do I?
**3** I love you; do I tell my teen this?
**4** I should praise my teen for using their initiative?

Here are 10 keynote winners circle of dreams tips to inspire your teenager

**1** Dream big
**2** What's his or her passion?
**3** Visualize the future, what will you be doing in 2 – 5yrs time
**4** Remember teenagers, "it takes guts, courage, and determination" to dream

**5** Write down your dreams and goals on paper
**6** Collect information that will help your teen decide what he or she wants

**7** Find a mentor who believes in your dream, take them out for lunch

## Every teenagers dream is inspired by different generations

**8** Parents support your teen to make good decisions

**9** Praise your teenager for the small steps & gains they have made towards their dream

**10** Inspire to influence loves is the answer.

<u>**A winner's mentality fuelled by action**</u>:" Be yourself--not your idea of what you think somebody else's idea of yourself should be." --**Henry David Thoreau**

No matter how many times you fall down in your life it matters how you rise up and get back up again you are the winner.

.

# Chapter 1 Notes

# Chapter 2

## Adults need to dare to dream again like kids. *"I Dream of good old days when I was kid."*

Those early days of 1960s growing up I remember my mum would sing to me every night she would cuddle me, hold me and make me feel important, "twinkle, twinkle little star, how I wonder how you are, up a above the world so high shining like a diamond in the sky", and that's how I felt, up above the world so high, that I could take on the whole wide world. She said to me Craig you can do anything in life if you put your mind to it, **"nothing is impossible, but is possible"**, you just have to work hard, or we can go the other way and do nothing for ourselves

One day I was watching a movie called 'The Alamo" about a man called Davey Crockett and a band of Indians, before the movie came on a man called Walt Disney, nice looking lean and with a moustache had appeared on the show. I asked my dad who he was, he my dad said, "was a rich man who owned a castle".

Twice a week I would sit down and watch this man Walt Disney, on the black and white TV and tell long tall stories about famous people doing well in America, at the beginning of each episode a song would come on the TV and it would go like this

> **"When you wish upon a star it makes no difference that who you are." Walt Disney**

For Walt to say , Wish upon a star and it makes no difference who you are , I was taking everything to heart and he really got me fired up, I start dreaming in my sleep, dreaming at school and around the dinner table, I was on my way to dreaming a dream for quite a while .

There is a need more so than ever, to dare to dream, especially in today's modern era. As adults we tend to use that word, busy, busy, busy, in our vocabulary, here are some of the excuses, ever heard them before; I will talk more in dept about excuses as you read through the book Winners Circle of dreams.

Questions you may ask yourself, why you won't dream at all.

# Adults need to dare to dream again like kids.

**1** I'm busy doing nothing with my time and still too busy,
**2** I have so many work commitments,
**3** I am busy with the kids,
**4** I'm too tired
**5** I will do it tomorrow
**6** I don't have a dream

Why do we find it so hard to dream as adults?

**"Is it society, do we feel that so many things in life are so important more than ourselves , we need to value and look at our own time ,sure we give and serve to others which is a good thing, but we never find time to ourselves".**

This is a trap so many adults get caught up with; really we tend to shoot ourselves in the foot. We can take charge of our dreams to believe, because if we don't what is the vision and direction we are heading down.

When we were kids, we all believed that we could do and achieve anything we wanted. We were all full of ambition, enthusiasm, and positivity. We personally remember our friends telling us, "We are going to be somebody, something ,someone, famous one day As kids we were always striving to be the best; those were fun times.

**We all as kids had big audacious dreams that we 100% believed that we were going to accomplish.**

However, as adults we grew older, those dreams got smaller, sadder, shrivelled and eventually died with regret. We also got distracted by other things that knocked us of our path to achieving great dreams

Does this really have to happen to us adults?

Yes it does, and it can happen, as you get older, you start interacting with individuals that aren't as ambitious, enthusiastic, and driven as you are. If your friends are having a bad day in their lives you tend to get stuck in a trap too, and you lose your ability to

## Adults need to dare to dream again like kids.

dream big, and everything and problem in life, starts to rub off on you. As the years go by, you now start to believe life should be a

Certain way. As adults we become close minded, kids aren't realist like adults, they are Imaginative dreamers.

**"If kids remained dreamers throughout their adult years, how will this world be? "Awesome"**

Most adults, who say they are realistic, love to point to examples like I'm someone who's 53 and can't make it into Xfactor because of their age, it's not possible for little old New Zealand, an island from the little pacific, who haven't got a chance to take the America's cup off America, "and New Zealand did", it's not possible to gain an education from college; many adults have gone back to school. The big secret with you, that you might not have known, "if that first big dream doesn't work out", dream another dream and many more , keep dreaming until the dreams are the right one for you , eventually the right one will work out!!!! As for looking for a job or starting your own business, same thing, you will have to put up with people saying the 'NO WORD" remember with every NO you are that much closer to a YES. Everything doesn't work out instantly, perfectly all the time, but don't let that stop you. Remember the immigrants of many lands they worked hard farmed the land, gave birth, and died for our country, but they had one thing in common, "The Big Dream", that the land they had come to was full of opportunities and their lives would be better. Commit and focus on the next big dream and go for it, you are bound to find one that will absolutely change your life.

**"Have you listen to yourself talk lately, we all do it , we talk about the dreams and all the things that went wrong , this is why as adults we don't dream big anymore. Because our mind set is clogged up with excuses".**

Remember what I just said, take the time to read about excuses later in the book, it so important for the benefit of yourself.

# Adults need to dare to dream again like kids.

The reason why kid's dreams are bigger than adults is simple; kids don't have the self-hang-ups s & big self-subconscious beliefs that adults have. Adults try not to dream big because they are afraid to fail again. The top 3 percent that own the world's wealth are all big dreamers that failed countless times; the only difference is they kept dreaming big until they found that something that worked. Successful adults are big dreamers.

As adults we need to start dreaming big dreams again. Our dreams should be like The Titanic one of the biggest cruise liner boats in the world.

**"We need a dream so big that we will do anything to climb aboard and cast off into open sea waters, and when it takes off, there's no stopping it".**

We as adults tend to pursue dingy dreams. Dreams that require no effort, you can just hop in and stay dormant

Dreaming give us as adults, hope and a purpose, that we are going to do something good for ourselves.
You can start dreaming again today, age is no barrier for big dreams, as an adult all you have to do is make time. For all of us to succeed, your dream and desire for success should be greater than fear of failure.

A dream can make so much of a difference in your life and again it's free.

Questions you need ask yourself.
**1** Can I make a change in my life?
**2** When is the right time?
**3** Is it easy to write a plan for my future?
**4** Can someone help me?
**5** When was the last time I dreamed of doing something great that's going to change my life, for me and my family?

Here are 7 keynote winners circle of dreams tips to start action dreaming again

# Adults need to dare to dream again like kids.

**1** As adults you need time away from work, friends, family
**2** Go to a place where there are no distractions.
**3** Turn the TV, cell phone off
**4** If time and money where not a problem, what could I be capable of doing
**5** Dream and think about you, if it's to be it's up to me
**6** Write down some dreams and goals that excite your interest
**7** Make a start, today is the day, not tomorrow, not next year, the time is now

These are 8 keynote winners circle of dreams tips to start your own dream shopping list today

**1** I want to dream about being a good husband/wife
**2** I want to dream about that new business or job
**3** I want to have the best relationship with my family
**4** I want to go on that holiday
**5** I want to be financially free
**6** I want the car, boat, and house.
**7** I want to be fit and healthy
**8** I want to be physically, spiritually, mentally strong

Give these suggestions a go; add on to your dream shopping list.

Have fun and start winning for you today.

<u>**A winner's mentality fuelled by action**</u>: "The price of greatness is responsibility." -**Winston Churchill**

No matter how many times you fall down in your life it matters how you rise up and get back up again you are the winner

# Christmas Dreams.

## The Christmas Eve dream.

Don't start me up about Christmas, I completely agree, media and technology has completely commercialized Christmas. I mean, it's always been a tradition to buy presents, but getting my kids toys in the 90's is different from getting your 2 yr old who is at day-care to 7 yr old at junior school a $500 iPad android, is how the world view this, is in the hands of the next generation of parents , we have become a commercial society more so , I know people and parents have the right to choose , or maybe people need to stop and think and relax a little , turn off the television, and other appliances and really think about, what the true meaning of Christmas is really all about ,spending time with our family and friends and thinking about just how thankful and blessed we are .

**"Can today's kids Christmas Dream survive in a commercial society, or has the childhood dream of Christmas and faith become non-event",** if the parent keep the true Christmas meaning & dream & spirit close to their hearts & alive with their stories",

they have been hand down through their grandparents, parents, the belief, dream, magic and power will be as strong as ever

I still believe , kids have always love Christmas ,I did ,so much I was one of those kids , I wished everyday was Christmas in my life, because Christmas meant so much to me and my family, it was a time we could all get together as a family ,Christmas was so magical we were all lost in the moment.

I remember so well One Christmas eve in 1968 night before Christmas my brothers and sister and I couldn't wait for Christmas day to come, mum was busy getting things all prepared for the big day ahead, dad had just got home from working at the hospital he would always bring food home for us, and on this one occasion he

# Christmas Dreams

had bought extra goodies home for Christmas , wow we were so overjoyed , just watching mum and dad put up the Christmas lights and decorations and our own personal stocking hanging up by the fire place all ready to go.

Dad and mum told all of us children to get down on our knees and prey , we said our prayers and gave thanks to heavenly farther, I can recall mum telling us smaller kids to go bed early, if we didn't Santa wouldn't come and visit us ,ok mum ,that night I tried to sleep. I could never forget this one night of excitement, what made it like this was, I had my big brothers and sister around me and although they were older than me,

> "They made me believe that Santa was so real, and that they did not steal or take away my Santa and Christmas dreams from me"

I was dreaming about the presents and my encounter with Santa, no doubt Santa arrived in my dreams and said hello to me .that night, I found it so hard to go to sleep because of the anticipation and over whelming enthusiasm, tinged with excitement the big day was so close and yet not within my grasps, was just around the corner. Finally Christmas day arrived ,I got up out of bed, run out into the sitting room , there were a pile of presents under the Christmas tree I opened my presents up and remember the Tonka toy truck , a cow boy cap gun , Bonanza and The High Chaparral were too big movies at the time ,all the kids in the neighbourhood wanted to cowboys or Indians. Family and I all saw Santa that morning; he had arrived on a truck and throwing out lollies around the neighbourhood, so as soon as we saw him I ran out to greet him.

I was a true winner at the end of the day, to me my dreams had all come true, a happy time with all my family, lunch, and dinner, and the presents.

As a parent today, I look back at that magical moment of the Christmas dream.

# Christmas Dreams

Questions you may ask yourself

1 What was my Christmas like when I was a kid?
2 Did I have a Christmas dream?
3 Is the true spirit of Christmas alive in me and my family?
4 What did I get for Christmas?
5 My magical Christmas moments, what were they?

Here are 6 keynote winners circle of dreams great tips for kids for Christmas

1 Talk with your kids and ask your kids what matters to them the most about Christmas.

2 Write down your kids Christmas & new year's dreams

3 Involve your kids in any and all Christmas preparation.

4 Let the kids put on a Christmas Event.

5 Get the kids disposable cameras so they can take photos of Christmas day.

6 If your kid is short of that something, example clothing shoes buy him or her, clothing or shoes for Christmas.

**A winner's mentality fuelled by action:** "Except and expect a positive thing, that is what it is, and that is what you will receive" – **Lori Hard**


No matter how many times you fall down in your life it matters how you rise up and get back up again you are the winner.

# The Birthday wish

Do you still care; I do, a birthday wish was like a dream to me.

Don't know about you guys going through and reading the last chapter, it just overwhelmed me and reminded me about the powerful gift of Christmas.

Do you remember the days when as little kids, a birthday was really something special; well nothing has changed, kids can get very excited. The two most important dates of any calendar year for kids' are:

**1** A child's birthday
**2** Christmas day

I know I was one of those kids, a birthday at the time meant so much to me; I couldn't wait for the day of days.

Dreaming Hoping and wishing ,what I would get was one thing, I know I dreamed about trucks and little match box toys and receiving a cricket set and soccer ball and spending my days with kids down the road. To me what meant most, on this particular birthday, was not about what I got and received, it was about, what I did and all the fun things I could get up to on the day? I even surprised myself with some of the things I would come up with.

**"I dreamed about what my day could be like."**
One of those dreams, was about catching and spiders and frogs, making a bow and arrow, it was the first time to try something new, **"Try to create your own birthday if you can, because you are the one who will always remember it the most"**

Those hot summers days of the late 1960s and early 70s,

they were such fond memories of just being a kid, I could do what I wanted to do, and be 'Huckle Berry Finn' for a day, on my travels with great expectations about how my day was going to fan out.

# The Birthday wish

So that summers morning I was full of energy got up out of bed mum was up to greet me with happy birthday ,I replied love you mum ,had a quick breakfast and made some sandwiches and headed off on my journey

This is how my day panned out. I had a written out a check list with every reason and desire to do all the things I said I would do, that I had dreamed about the night before.

My birthday dream wish list

## 1 Blackberry picking

So my brother Brian his friend Gus and I set off and went at the back roads of Collins road country blackberry picking on the outskirts of the Hamilton The blackberries were so big, black and beautiful to eat, I guess we ate far more than our fair share and what we took home, we couldn't resist how plentiful and succulent they tasted, well the rest is history, I had taken some of mums old glass jam jars from home and filled them up with blackberries and was looking forward to the smell of blackberry pie.

## 2 Bows and Arrows

Later on morning we moved on, Gus & my brother Brian were experienced campaigners at making bows and arrows they were like the robin hoods of the neighbourhood, as kids everybody would look up at these two as heroes, these kids that would try their hands at anything, most times the things they tried, would pay off, if something was wrong, they would try and try again until they got it right, I ended up cutting up tree branches and fern sticks and making the bow and the arrows, I had bought with me my own string and a little pocket knife, there was plenty of space to test out the bow and arrow; I was so overjoyed when I tested my bow and arrow.

When I shot my arrow it actually went further than my brother and his friend Gus.

# The Birthday wish

## 3 Catching the biggest wolf spiders we could find

Lunch time and those sandwiches came in handy, as I was starting to gain an appetite I ended up sharing those sandwiches with the boys .I ask them, "where was your lunch", and **they said Craig, you should be grateful you are coming with us, we are teaching you a few life skills here, so those sandwiches belong to all of us, "we are a team aren't we".** "I guess", watch us and learn from us how to catch this wolf spider they are pretty fast. I pulled another jar out of my bag, and gave it to my brother, he said look and see how Gus catches them.

There is a way of catching the wolf spider in and on the outside of its web. Gus placed the biggest part of the glass jar behind the web and the lid in front; he then quickly bought the two together without injuring the big wolf spider. He cleared the web off around the rim and shakes the jar up so the spider can't climb out on one of its webs. The spider dropped out of the web Gus holding the big glass jars under the spider and using a little help and push with a stick the spider fell, into the jar. Was I scared? Yes I was, these spiders, were big black, beautiful, with yellow stripes, hairy but so harmless I was happy just having my one spider in my jar, my brother and Gus ended up catching 6 spiders, later that day we let our spiders go.

## 4 Catching tadpoles and frogs.

The most exciting part of the day, was yet to come , as we were crossing farm land on the outskirts of Hamilton not yet a big city , more a major farming community but filled with lushes pastures after all it was in the heart of Waikato country , houses were going up everywhere ,we lived in one of the first built government houses that my parents can be proud of ,owning their house.

Gus, Brian and I, had spotted a trench pond on a farm on the back drop of Melville; I can recall jumping over the farm fence, into the paddock. As we got closer to the pond, the pond looked semi dry, but still had water in it. It was shallow and looked kind of murky.

# The Birthday wish

I was over the moon and couldn't wait for the moment to hold a frog in my hand , Gus had bought a little net with him , he said to me, this is what you catch tadpoles with ,and if there are tadpoles, here are adult frogs around , tadpoles are actually baby frogs if you don't know .

Another thing Craig is you have to be quiet, because frogs can sense people are around, they can get scared, once you have spotted a frog. it is likely that the frog will jump back into the water if he hears you, Gus and Brian knew what they were doing, I didn't know a thing, Gus said the key is to force them onto dry land or into a corner so the frog can't escape.

What we will do is cause a distraction, corners them down one side of the trench pond, approach the frog in the water if possible. We blocked off any escape and continued to force the frog inland, and use our hands to snatch up the frog. We attempted to use the net and other jar and with our hands prepared to get ready.

Well the boys hopped in the water and their strategy worked, they had caught with their bare hands, a big black bull frog

That afternoon we had caught several frogs green, black, brown ones, the boys also had shown me a way to catch the frogs in the water, they said you could feel with your hands, the holes under the water on the side of the pond, and put you hand into the hole and you would find a frog, I tried and it worked

I will always remember this day ,I achieved all I set out to do, I had lived my dream for a day which made me a winner , mum was happy she cooked blackberry pie, and I had fun catching frogs and spiders, and making my bow and arrow.

**"The key difference to become successful for a day and make it memorable, was I had other people to help me achieve my dream"**

I thank my brother Brian and Gus ,I reflect back on how they had taught me a few lessons, that was is all about life skills, working as a team, you have to get out and take action. I ended up a winner after all.

# The Birthday wish

Questions you may ask yourself
1 As a kid, what did I dream about for my birthday?
2 Did I celebrate my birthday by doing something different?
3 Have I told my kids what I got up to on my birthday when I was their age?

Here are 6 keynote tips for kid's birthday.
1 Try doing something different.
2 Create easy ideas
3 Keep the party simple
4 Write a birthday list
5 Invite your best friends to Theme party
6 Make sure they are all winners

**<u>A winner's mentality fuelled by action</u>:** "No one has ever become poor by giving." -**Anne Frank**


No matter how many times you fall down in your life it matters how you rise up and get back up again you are the winner.

- **YOU ON THE Big Dreamers LIST.**

The biggest dreamers in the world

Here is a list of some biggest list of dreamers who have help shape the world

And you could be next.

Teachers
Scientists
Writers
Doctors
Lawyers
Dentists
Leonardo DaVinchi
Community workers
Social worker
Poets
Vincent Van Gogh
Tom O'Neil NZ Author/ Motivational speaker
Actors
Mickey mouse
John Williams
Santa
Church pastors
Authors
Scientist
Paraplegics
Bill gates USA Founder Windows
Steve Jobs USA Founder Apple
Peter Jackson
Martin Luther king
Walt Disney USA
Trade me NZ founder Sam Morgan
Google US

# Are you on the big dreamers list

The Beetles
Wal-Mart USA
Elvis priestly
Amway
Herbal life
KFC
AVON
Thomas Edison
Sir Edmond Hillary
Benjamin Franklin
Subway
Burger king
Kathmandu NZ
Napoleon Hill
Mike Pero NZ
Lisa Carrington NZ Sports Woman
Valarie Adams NZ shot put thrower
Face book
YouTube
Mc Donald's US food giant
Beyonce singer US
C d Walden Author The Book Winners Circle of Dreams

All of these people in big dreamers club had one thing in common, they dreamed a big dream and pursued with desire, determination and doing the unthinkable to become very successful .this is what big dreamers do, they are determined to plant a seed of action & sacrifice everything and commit to see the abundance fruits of their dream flourish, become reality and successful.

**"You the see big dreamers club overcame the challenges' storms, obstacles, never give up and stuck around to fight for the win".**

## Are you on the big dreamers list

Ray croc, Steve jobs, bill gates and many other people weren't dreaming about winning lotto and waiting for the easy way out , waiting for the ship to arrive and scream out, save me, give me a hand out, their dreams became real and started to take shape when they started to believe it was possible. We all have been given the gift and power inside of us to dream .All we have to do is set our sail and navigate our position and head to the destination where our heart will take us , there could be storms along the way but that's the beauty of the challenge of following your heart's desire, I truly believe the future can be very bright, and better than our past, how bright, I always look at the stars in the sky, and there are so many, each little star has it own unique unknown story to tell .close your eyes and dream about the stars, reach out and pick one, name it ,believe in it and then tell a story.

**"You know there are so many dreams, that should have been written in ones life, that could have been written on this list, and yet those dreamers started their dream race with a roar, but gave up and failed, to end their race".**

I truly believe we can start a fresh today, and work our way towards writing our name into the history book of our own life and leave a legacy

What's holding you back today is it fear of failure that you dread, are you passionate about your dream, is your dream the right one for you, don't worry dream more than 1 dream , find the dream that suits you today, it's not about what's happened in the past, your dreams are determined on your future out comes .

**Questions you may ask yourself**

**1** If I knew I could not fail and win today, tomorrow, and forever, what would I be capable of?

**2** If I could dream big, doing something amazing in my life what would it be?

# Are you on the big dreamers list

Here are 6 keynote tips to join the winners circle dream list.
**1** Start dreaming and believing today
**2** Decide and discover what your destiny is and where it will take you.
**3** What's holding you back?

**4** Are you ready to set sail, cross the start line, and head to your destination?

**5** How prepared are you to weather the turbulent storms of life that will blow your way, and rock your boat from time to time?

**6** The rewards are the greatest for those who dreamed a dream pursued endured and finished to the end of their race

**<u>A winner's mentality fuelled by action</u>:** "You have to be burning with "an idea, or a problem, or a wrong that you want to right." If you're not passionate enough from the start, you'll never stick it out." **- Steve Jobs**

No matter how many times you fall down in your life it matters how you rise up and get back up again you are the winner.

# CHAPTER 2 NOTES

# Chapter 3

## • The dentist who excited me with dreams.

Back in February 1990 it was early afternoon , my brother in law and his wife at the time, had called us up at short notice , about some opportunity, I didn't have a clue about ,what they were going on about ,I could feel their excitement through the phone, "we have something that could change your life" so they said believe it or not, at that time , my mum recently had passed away, and we had purchased the family home .

I was working for the post office and only on one income; my wife Angela was busy with our two children Alisha and Jeremy

I wanted to say no to my brother in-law and try and find all ways and the excuses under the sun for them to make the appointment not happen ,truth was I was naïve and very sceptical**,** they actually were doing me a favour, but at the time I couldn't see it, ,and what they believed in, from their hearts . Ever tried going to the movies, I went and saw a **dream movie of 1979 called Star Wars** 6 or 7 times, first thing I did after the movie, I told all my friends who hadn't seen the movie to go and see it.

**"That year of 79 good news travels fast worldwide and those so call dreamers and creators of the star wars epic George lucus and Steven Spielberg won** "**an Oscar, how about that"**

I get the picture, my brother in law was excited about a dream opportunity that he had seen and heard and he wanted to share his good news with my wife and I and friends .and so the story goes, in the end, we said yes. I started ringing around to friends and ask them around to our place, some came, others didn't, so what, the meeting was scheduled, That late afternoon, we were waiting for my in-laws to arrive, they didn't show up on this day because they couldn't find a baby sitter, so they couldn't make it over from Tauranga, they rang us back and said sorry we can't make it, but no worries, we have found someone else who could show the opportunity, you still want to.

## The dentist who excited me with dreams.

go ahead, yep we said lets go with the flow, so we set up house, we put a couple of chairs out in the lounge along with light refreshments .

At 530pm our own friends had arrived waiting in anticipation we had a full house and a sleek looking BMW car had pulled up in our drive way, this man and woman got out of the car , there was something about this couple that was so different, their smile big, bright ,beautiful.

The couple had just walked in the door. Along with them came a long white board , and everyone went quiet, was it because john was lean and tall looked, intellectual, with trendy glasses, Helen was her name she looked very beautiful and radiant and they both dressed well to do.

Every one sat down on their chairs, John and Helen set up the white board ,then said hello everyone hope you enjoy your selves tonight, we have an opportunity, we would like to share with you tonight. I could hear my friends mummer to themselves, what is it, hurry up, get to the point, this will be interesting, I could see they were so anxious along with my wife and I to find out what it was they had to say.

John and Helen ask everyone to 1 introduce themselves, 2 what they did for a living. So we all one by one introduced ourselves to each other, even though we all knew one and other as friends.

John and Helen said, now we know who you are; we will tell you what we do for a living.

We live in Auckland, Helen and I am professional dentists. You couldn't hear a pin drop of a whisper from anyone; yes he said we are dentist, just like all of you we work, so tonight is a time to share this exciting opportunity to all of you

Let me start of by saying and writing down the words **"D.R.E.AM-TIME-MONEY to be successful at this opportunity you must have a dream".**

## The dentists who excited me with dreams.

If money and time weren't a problem ever thought about what you would do, some friends yelled out, I love my job. Let me tell you again if time & money weren't a problem think about it seriously

I am going to draw a big circle below time & money and call it the dream circle

What I want you to do is tell me what it is you would like to do or want.

So we all started to put our dreaming and thinking caps on and to our amazement here was a list of some of the things that john put on the board

*New house.
*New car
*Big birthday
*Travel
*Clothes for the family
*More $$$ more income
*Health insurance
*Boat
*Pay of the mortgage.
*Wealthy.
*Financially free.

We were all surprised with what we had come up with, and we were all filled in excitement, that we had already achieved those so called dreams which seemed so close and imbedded in our minds.

John and Helen had got our reasons out of us, the dreams we could see with our own eyes, written in plain black and white on the board.

John asks me and my friends, what's stopping us now from achieving our dreams.

We were just stunned, we really didn't have a clue, what to say except, how fast can we get those things done.

John and Helen said to us, if you want those things it takes:

# The dentists who excited me with dreams.

"A Reason why
How bad do want that dream
You must have Commitment
Attitudes second to none"
You help other people get what they want, they will help you get what you want
Follow our company system of tapes books and functions

John and Helen excited me enough, about all those dreams that night, as for my friends some of them said things like., I haven't got time , I don't know if I can do it, I'm too busy with my family, I don't have enough money to get into business.

My friends were allowed their right to opinion and choice, and still I love my friends to bits.

Angela and I learnt a lot from this particular night, which will stay with us forever. This man and woman who had come to dinner changed our thoughts and lives forever

**"John and Helen made us dream of the possibilities through a big dream"**

Goals, desire, reason, and eagerness and action, they believed any ones dream could become a reality on the path to success. John and Helen mentioned that night also how they dreamt that computers and a thing call network marketing and the world wide web were going to revolutionize how we buy our goods and service ,also how we could keep our fulltime jobs and earn a living ,work part-time and earn a fortune

Questions you may ask yourself.
**1** Does a stranger, paint a picture; have merit and value in my life.
**2** How often do you get strangers showing you an opportunity?
**3** What would my reasons be for me taking up the offer?

## The dentists who excited me with dreams.

Here are 6 keynote tips about dreams and opportunities.

**1** Be open minded to dreams and opportunities

**2** Guard your mind and heart if hyped opportunities are too good to be true...

**3** You can be naïve and very sceptical if you don't know much about the business opportunities.

**4** Do your research and ask questions about the opportunity, company, and business venture

**5** Seek advices from people who have been successful in the industry, you wish to pursue

**6** What is the reason and risk factor for taking on the business opportunity, will it take me and my family forward and into the future or will it send me backwards.

**<u>A winner's mentality fuelled by action:</u>**"Sometimes the heart sees what is invisible to the eye." **-H. Jackson Brown, Jr.**

No matter how many times you fall down in your life it matters how you rise up and get back up again you are the winner.

- **Dreams are possibilities waiting to evolve.**

Isn't funny how dreams become reality 20 YEARS ago, that network company that john and Helen talked to my friends and I about was called **Amway** it has evolved into a world-wide global company and is still positioned as one of the strongest fortune 500 companies in America today, Amway today have so many diamond distributors, millionaires who are financially free and independent. Dreams are like opportunities waiting to evolve, and the great thing about this is

**"Every dream and opportunity has a story to tell because they came from nothing to something and then progressed into reality"** This is what the winner's circle of dreams is all about, there are winners inside all of us as people, all we have to do is activate the dream that's been waiting to explode inside of us, and write your story and sign your signature to success,

Just remember the countless dreams that are just waiting to be conquered.

But first, what do you want. Which direction are you heading in, how do I get there.

Did you know many dreams and visions "**go unfulfilled and become impossible because the dreamer or visionary didn't have time for them**"?
How many stories do you know or songs that go unwritten because the writers couldn't find the time to write them or didn't cross the finish line,
ask yourself the question It is best to die with regret or with all your dreams, goals and ideas, used up locked away in the cupboard and gathering dust, along with your stories not written and finished.

If we take a look at the world today the dreams of many makers of inventions, medical advancement, and cures for cancer, technology and major companies have evolved and leap forged with possibilities into the future.

## Dreams are possibilities waiting to evolve.

Transforming the path from process, to concept and systems to practical creation and over view requires an understanding science and familiarity with current technologies; both scientist and engineers must have a big dream with vision to see beyond the world as it is today.

Utilizing knowledge and tools of today with dreams of tomorrow determine and shape the world of the future.

Today we have such powerful handheld devices as computers, the information hub of World Wide Web, iPod or the Blackberry, and discovered new drugs that have revolutionized medicine, and the future coming generation of Sir Richard Branson Virgin space ship travel. Not long ago, each of these was any more than a dream, but today each is a reality and possibility thanks to the vision of talented people who had the power to dream big. We do not know what our world will look like 30 or 60 or 1000 years from now, but we do know that whatever new dreams, vision, possibilities will appear, they will certainly shape our future.

**"Many have failed where few have succeeded, are prepared to leave a legacy to inspire and influence others into the future".**

I can say I was stuck in a 1 bed room flat and my daughter sleeping on the floor and lack of money, I do thank heavenly farther for all he has given me, what drives me and keeps me going is the power of the big dream, I visualize the amazing possibilities ahead now and in the future, holding the book winners circle of dreams in my hand, and speaking, inspiring to influence people from all over the world.

Many people need to pick up on their scattered dreams and ignite them again, maybe you are the next inventor of software or hardware technology or the next big best movie director or could discover the next breakthrough in medical science, maybe you have a dream to help others in this world, who are less fortunate than you

**"The power of big dreams is its ability to show us what we are capable of".**

# Dreams are possibilities waiting to evolve.

## A scattered dream simply means you have not yet dreamed the way to get there yet..."

Dream the destination and then dream the process on how to get there.

Forget about the impossible dream; take action today think about what can be achieved, and what if it is possible

Questions you may ask yourself

**1** Do I have those X factor dreams and possibilities, qualities, skills, attitude waiting to evolve, inside of me?

**2** How many of those X factor dreams and possibilities, qualities, skills, attitude can evolve into reality?

Here are 5 keynote tips about dreams and opportunities

**1** How do you view the world and how we have evolved today?

**2** Even those scattered dreams are ready to evolve; all you have to do is reactivate them again.

**3** Do you have that reason and burning desire in you, to make a difference in today's world?

**4** Write your story, leave a legacy, and sign your signature to success

**5** What will future generations say about you in 10 -20 -30 years' time?

<u>**A winner's mentality fuelled by action:**</u>" If you're going to dream and show case your story to the world, make sure you have a big dream & a big story, or none at all." - **Joseph Campbell**

No matter how many times you fall down in your life it matters how you rise up and get back up again you are the winner.

- ## I was dreaming of Xfactor 2013, just do it?

## X factor New Zealand 2013

When I started to write this book I thought about some, type of thing in my personal life .that I have always dreamed about, and have never been able to do until now, guess what I have always had a passion for music and singing, ever since I was a kid, I loved singing and imitating little Donny Osmond & Michael Jackson, check them out on YouTube, every chance id get to sing in the bath, at church or just in front of my family, it made me feel good inside, a burst of raging fuel like passion burning inside my body. Over the years I have been singing at funerals and weddings and mostly family gatherings, never before have I sung in front of professionals and now after all these years the time has come,

> "It is better to find that something, you love to do, than being told what to do, there is no time like the present, I have that 1 chance to impress for success, as **Elvis once quoted; he said "it's now or never".**

Well I have now dedicated this chapter in pursuit of Xfactor New Zealand 2013, I truly believe in 2013 that as you read this chapter that you will follow me, I will hold your hand every step of the way, from day one. Such as my audition with the producers of the show and hopefully follow up with the processes to performance and what is required to go to the next level. Here I am at 53 and already people have said Craig either you are stupid, or you're outrageously mad and crazy in mind. I love it when people put a limitation on you and cage you up. People tend to forget they under estimate you and your capabilities.

Here are some of the things been said?
**1** You're too old
**2** You can't sing
**3** You don't have the Xfactor

# I was dreaming of Xfactor 2013, just do it?

4 Looking for young people sorry
5 You are wasting your time
6 There are so many people who are better than you already
Remember people, **"this is my dream and not yours"**, in today's society , the comparisons & negativity is all so alive & around us , many people want to dream big , but their dreams are shattered and scattered & turned small & shrunk, lost in fear of what someone , somebody .family or friends ,might say, so they live with the fear of failure.

I look forward to learning how far my dream, purpose, passion, determination, to be the best I can be, will take me, all I can do is ask of myself of me, and even if I don't get to the next round, I have won already, by achieving my dream and going into the competition with the action of today, **"I have nothing to lose and everything to gain".** So follow this chapter I hope I can inspire myself first, and then you, to take the next step,

**"The best advice I can give you, "is follow your passion, hold your dream close to your heart, if I can do it, you can too",**

Believe and you will be amazed at what it is you can achieve. I am so excited Today is Tuesday January 29$^{th}$ 2013 this morning I am leaving Tauranga and I am going back to my home town of Hamilton, back to the place where I was born.**For me I know today is going to be a great day and I am looking forward to my audition, this is that something I have dreamed about, I have always wanted to do , now "if its to be its going to take me" , I have to pull out my A game and be** mentally strong in mind ,prepared not just to sing and audition but to explode and take control of my moment of destiny, I was talking to my wife and she said "give it a go", what have you got to lose, today, I said, I am in control of my dream, "virtually nothing", I'm living my

# I was dreaming of Xfactor 2013, just do it?

dream for me and no one knows how I feel but me. So here I am **I'm going for it, I'm going to make success happen and not wait for it to come to me,** as they say, put on a performance, inspire to influence the judges so they will be left speechless, show myself, what I am capable of from power within me. So I head off to my home town of Hamilton with my water, good clothes, prepared mentally and physically and ready to roll, I am so excited not nervous at all. But I don't want to say two much about confidence at the moment. I dropped Angela off at her course at 7.50am

I prayed to heavenly father, for a great day, safe journey to Hamilton.

While travelling over kaimais to Hamilton I could see it was going to turn out a beautiful day , then started to visualize my dream in my mind, and picture me singing a song called **Shower me with your love by artists surface** , I had a back-up plan as well ,because I knew , I would have to have a second song ready as well, called **let's stay together by artist al green** , started to sing ,I was certain that these were the songs I was going to perform to the producers.

My voice my mind was ready in tune with each other. The performance result was great.

At 9:45am I cruised into Hamilton and parked in Hood Street car park, then walked down to the Meteor Theatre in Anglesey Street and there was a huge line of hopefuls waiting and I ended up waiting in line at 10.20am, well talk about hype, I new it was going to be an entertaining and long day, waiting in the hot sun, I mean scorching hot! But lucky I had my water bottle, and best of all I used my brain and brought a mini umbrella, that was enough to keep the heat stroke away, that kept me comfortable for the day.

Many contestants complained about the time it took to get into the theatre and the heat. Amongst all of that, to get us through, was the

# I was dreaming of Xfactor 2013, just do it?

entertainment and the talent of musicians singing and practicing their songs, so much talent, but limited places in the auditions.

I had my share of comments, people telling me how good this and that person is, and you could hear the critics also, "was I going to listen to negative comments", I had a choice, but I decided in my own mind "no way"? I was here for a purpose to dream the dream reach the target and finish my race, it was always up to me and no one else but me.

At 1.45pm I registered signed the audition papers, I had been waiting outside for 3.15 hours, it was worth it. However one slight dilemma I had, I didn't have photo id. The girl asked me if I was a New Zealand citizen, I said yes, I spoke in Maori, Ki ora and I went on through to the waiting rooms inside.

Inside the venue was a whole different atmosphere, the pressure was on for a lot of the contestants , I saw some sad faces leaving the venue in tears ,I was given bracelet number 3829 and the guy said this is your audition number please when I call out your number you will go to the next room and wait for your audition , I didn't panic or stress out .I had 40min up my sleeve before I was called to audition ,what did I do with my 40 min, I had given to me, I went outside went for a walk , talk to some people and practice my songs ,the biggest thing I did was to relax.

2. 40pm call up 3829, well this was the moment, I got up out of my chair and started to walk through to the audition waiting room 1 there were 3 other contestants waiting before me, we were 2 minutes apart of each other.

I watched two guys go in and out in 2 minutes, and then another guy went in at that moment. I said to myself. I am ready to hit my target, I started the race, now "how do I want to finish my race", I wanted to finish my race with excellence, and then the last guy came out, he seemed happy but I didn't hear back from him, as to a result.

Well my moment had arrived; I put on my jacket and walked into the audition room

# I was dreaming of Xfactor 2013, just do it?

A lady was waiting, I said, hello how are you today, and she said good, she ask me what have you got to show me today? I said, I am going to sing "Barbra Streisand, The way we were" She said let me hear what you got Ok I said. So with 2 quick breaths I sung. I felt great and gave everything I had to give with lots of feeling and love. She said, 'Donald you were really good" I felt the song and the storyline in my heart great Donald, I will say yes Donald you are through to the next room, I fell to the floor and said thank you, and I said are you sure? She said, Donald you are through to the next room full of producers. I was whisked away to the next room straight away without even a break. Then room 2 opened and sitting there were 2 guys 1 of the guys Andrew was the main producer of Xfactor NZ.

The producers said to me straight away, show us what you've got. I am going to sing The THEME from The Way We Were from Barbra Streisand. I really didn't know how the guys would take it, a guy singing a divas song. I started to sing and performed how I performed in room one, they stop me, they said Donald guess what, that was wonderful and great, waiting for the verdict, they said yes, you are through to the next round, I questioned the producer's and said is that a maybe or yes and Andrew said your audition is a yes, go home to your family and tell them the great news have a wonderful week.

I was so overjoyed with excitement and over the moon and also so humble and thanked heavenly father for helping me get through the day.

When I got home and told my wife and kids what had happen, my wife believed in me always, she had the biggest smile on her face, and as for the kids they were shocked.

It all starts with believing in you and your big dream first.

# I was dreaming of Xfactor 2013, just do it?

Here is 10 keynote tips to help you with your first audition
**1** Be on time
**2** Block out negativity
**3** Relax
**4** Be positive have courage
**5** Be greater than your best
**6** Believe in you, I can do it
**7** Check your processes, audition paperwork, audio check, and sheet music.
**8** Practice your song visually and mentally, warm your vocals.
**9** When you sing your song you are telling a story
**10** Inspire and influence the judges and audience so they feel the story in your in the song

So readers Now I am through to the 2 round march $2^{nd}$ 2013, Singing in front of the Xfactor judges, something I have never done before, what happens from here, it's all about the possibilities, of, how far my dream will take me.

And if I don't precede to the next level its ok I am still a winner.

# Xfactor Audition day Auckland march $2^{nd}$ 2013

Well its Saturday morning march $2^{nd}$ 2013, nothing is going to stop me from achieving my dream.

Do you know **"There are things that happen in your life, that are out of your hands, that you have no control of?"**

One of those things that has happened was, I was coming down with the flu ,yes a sore throat, I didn't ask for this to happen to me , but it happened and it's not worth it stressed out,

Myself, Angela, Jessie, and I left Tauranga 7am and arrived in Auckland at 930am, that morning we arrived at my daughter's home at Mt Eden in Auckland.

# I was dreaming of Xfactor 2013, just do it?

At 1230pm I registered at the Xfactor desk at the sky convention centre.

Im not going to make any excuses about how the day panned out, all I know is, what I said I set out to do, what I wanted to do, and that was to stand on stage and be in front of the judges of Xfactor.

I could have told the producers to cancel my audition, but I didn't, I believed my show must go on regardless of my circumstances.

You see even though I had the flu, I could of made two choices cancel my audition or carry on,

If I had cancelled out, I would not have achieved the ultimate goal and experience and feelings of the dream,

In the end I got to go on stage and in front of the judges. Just walking out in front of the live audience and in front of the judges was so electric and unbelievable.

The judges asked me a few questions, I told them I was writing a book about winners circle of dreams, they asked me about the book I said the book is about the winning we all have inside of us, we are all winners, and we just have to believe. I have dreamed about this one moment and it's finally here I am a winner for being here on the big stage.

I didn't get through to the next round, I loved the judges' comments I sang the theme song from The way we were, accapella style, I tried my best, but in the end the judges said I chose the wrong song choice, there was nothing wrong with my voice and Mel thought I was creepy, I can live and handle their comments. There are times when things don't go the way you want them to be, you learn from

the experience to take you forward in your life and mould you to be a better and stronger person .

# I was dreaming of Xfactor 2013, just do it?

Some advice I can pass over to you is,

**"I achieved my dream" and I was true to me , no matter how your dream turns out , and on the inside of you, you know you are happy with what you did, then no one can take away your moment of glory". CD Walden**

To participate in Xfactor was a great achievement and great experience I will never forget.

Here are some of the Highs and Lows of Xfactor.

H  I was **1 of 6000 people** who auditioned throughout New Zealand.
L  Don't get **sick**, stay fit and healthy
H  I got into the top **300** auditions
L  If you can't handle **critics** don't enter
H  Got to achieve my dream to sing **in front of the Xfactor judges**
L  Make sure you **pick the song that's right for you,** know your song

H  I didn't win Xfactor, I did my best and still **I won my own race.**

L  This is your first time at Xfactor and the judges say no and you don't succeed then **you can always try again**

Hey if you are contemplating doing Xfactor give it ago, you never know where your dream will take you.

Remember once again, please if you missed out go back and give it another go, you are the winner for trying

**A winners mentality fuelled by action:** "Don't let life discourage you; everyone who got where he or she was, is had to begin where he or she was." -**Richard L. Evans.**

No matter how many times you fall down in your life it matters how you rise up and get back up again you are the winner.

- **My dad said to me "You know it's never too late"**

I have had people say to my wife and I, I don't know how you 2 do it, you been married for 26 years, "what your secret", we are firm believers of faith and hope, we love one and other, our marriage is

like a business, it needs nurturing the more you put in, the more you get out of it, so go ahead start spicing up your life with big dreams it's never too late to achieve what's possible

Those of you who have been reading this book so far, to this point ,may have noticed something   No matter how old you are, what your life situation you are in right now, you can change today and look towards a brighter future.

Talk about change there an insert about change you need to read and come across later on in the book.

You know it's never too late to do the things you have always wanted to do, why do people have a so called bucket, wish list tucked away somewhere, and then they bring it out in 20 years' time, say honey, we haven't done this before, I have always wanted to do that, but I never found the time, you see people, they want to achieve, tick off all those so call things that they love doing, but never got around to doing it.

I said I was going to be a motivational speaker and write a book called winner circle of dreams and at 52 who ever thought that would happen or could happen, as they say it's me and only me, I am accountable to me, because I breathe and live the big dream and I see myself so much closer to the finish line

You have to Go for your dreams ,no one else will believe you have what it takes but you, its, never too late to follow them, and you wont be disappointed honestly I have always wanted to do Xfactor NZ 2O13 it took guts, action, desire,

# My dad said to me "You know it's never too late"

I didn't care about what age I was, or in fact how I looked, or even the end result. It was all about the dream and passion I had inside of me, I won for me, and that's all that matters

## "Go ahead do anything you like, it's not too late, who said that"?

"yourself or friends" , I know I wanted to try out for Xfactor and I achieved what I set out to do, just be you, want to be a Singer/performer, teacher business, actor at 75 years old, pastor, live to 105, in a TV commercial, go for it! Never give up, don't let others say it too late to do anything new in your life , **you know what you are capable of , no one will know more so than you** ,you need to be strong and stay away from negative parasites in your life who say the "no" word . There are thousands of people millions who want to dream about doing something great and wonderful in their lives and who are trying so hard! So if you have the dream ,tell yourself by saying, today is the first new day , I am going to try something new in my life ,it's that something that I always wanted to do, like I want to be the best person I can be, I am going to go to the gym and get fit ,but I thought it was too late in my life to do it, guess what, im going to give it a go, what have I got to lose , man I am so excited about my dreams ,the futures so bright ,look at all of the possibilities ahead for me  ,all I need to succeed is the change of mind set, heart, reason, desire ,action, drive, commitment, dedication. You and I both know you'd feel better about yourself if you try, because if you give up you're always going to wonder what could have been. Pursue your passion for you to win and doing something you love!

These words my farther spoke to me , there is a price to pay for trying and  it's never too late to try your hand at anything in life , referring that dad knew I was good at sport when I was I kid ,I loved, running, cricket ,and rugby. You have two choices, 1 you are either good at something you love, 2 or you are bad at doing something you hate, my dad when he got the chance, would come outside in the backyard and bowl to

# My dad said to me "You know it's never too late"

me with the cricket ball and help me with my batting, he gave me 4 key tip's 1 Gain in self-confidence, 2 keep learning and practice, practice, practice 3 believe in yourself, 4 always show great attitude, because who cares what other people think about you. You can't please everyone, don't let the bad things people say, take you down, let it make you stronger. You know what you are capable of; no one knows that, but you, Continue chasing your dreams, what people are going to remember, is your effort and trying, no matter, what others say to you. You can do anything

Remember it's never too late to do anything it just takes belief, vision, eagerness, courage, hard work.

Questions you may ask yourself

**1** What is that one special thing I have always wanted to do?

**2** How can I make it happen?

**3** Does my dream need nurturing like a successful marriage, company, business.

**Here are 10 keynotes "it's never too late tips"**

**1** It's never too late to do anything; trouble is you have to be at the start line early to begin your race.

**2** It's never too late to try something you love doing
**3** It's never too late to believe in you
**4** It's never too late to achieve your level of expectation
**5** It's never too late age is not a barrier.
**6** It's never too late to forgive and forget
**7** It's never too late to plan for a brighter future
**8** It's never too late to serve others
**9** It's never too late to find happiness
**10** It's never too late to love.

<u>**A winners mentality fuelled by action**</u>: "Success is almost totally dependent upon drive and persistence. The extra energy required to make another effort or try another approach is the secret of winning." – **Denis Waitley**

# Chapter 3 Notes.

# Chapter 4

## We are born to win

We are born to win just do it
"You have a winners spirit" Dad and Mum said ,you have to go out and make something of your life, now I know what they meant , you see nothing in life will ever be given or handed to you on a plate, if you really want something in life just do it , I am a firm believer , I know our creator has blessed each and every one of us here on this earth, we are gifted in our own unique and wonderful way ,we are born to win ,and not made to lose ,you have to go out and get what you want, and once you know what you want the winner inside of you will always surface & project on the outside of you ,the truth is, if we are to have any chance of winning ourselves, we have to work on the winning from inside of us first, we have to start writing our own story, starting with the process of cleaning out our negative thoughts and filling them with a new mind-set of positive thoughts, faith, and, belief. How can we dream about the future if our mind and our creativity thoughts cannot function properly and locked away in the prison of negativity?

So many people don't think they can make a change; they stay in their self-pity mode. Be like a rhino get tough and hard skinned and stop feeling sorry for you.

Throughout my life time, and there have been so many I can recall, we tend to think, "why do I feel this way" or what's happening to me, why is life not so good to me. Why is there so much adversity in the moments, I don't need all of this, im not worthy, no one cares about me, im broke, im in debt and don't know how to get out of a rut.

Why we may ask is, because we pondering over ourselves with, that I feel sorry for myself, bad attitude factor, maybe. We are all good at blaming each other for their demise, and not our own, this is so true. It takes discipline and the courage to look at ourselves in

# We are born to win

In which, we may not like what we see. In society today we have been conditioned to evaluate and judge everything we experience. Pretty much without realizing it, we take these beliefs to another level in our own mind set and lives.

I can honestly tell you now; we are born to win just do it
So what we really need to do, is take a look at ourselves in the mirror and change our mind set of thinking, say god help me through these times .good or bad, negative or positive or good dream or bad dream, do I work today, or do I not, we all call this the power of thoughts and transformation processes and the performances leading up to a great choice, we weren't born to lose, we are born to win. From today onwards start winning today, and just do it.

Do you really want to know **the difference between winning and losing mentality, losers don't fix bad problems, winners cease the opportunities** rise from a bad problem, change their mind-set and attitude quickly, find a solution, turn them around for good, to make a gain to go forward in their lives

If you are sick, get healthy, go jogging, and then you are born to win, just do it.

If you are overweight, change your diet, then you are born to win, just do it.

If you have no job, get a job, then you are born to win, just do it.

If you have no skills at all, learn to acquire new skills, and then you are born to win, just do it.

We have limitless abundance of opportunities in front of us, yet most people can't see when we are still looking back at our past, living amongst our old habits and we settle for second best and live with the what ifs

IF your parent, family, son, daughter, grandparents relationship is in bad shape, transform and resolve your problems, Then you are born to win, just do it.

# We are born to win

Questions you may ask yourself.
1 Am I born to win? yes
2 Do I have the winner's spirit in me? yes
3 What's holding me back from winning? you


Here are 6 quick powerful tips on how you are born to win
1 Change your mind set today, just do it?
2 Write down I can do, instead of I can't, just do it.
3 Turn of the negative rubbish on TV, just do it.
4 Get rid of the doom and gloom, just do it?
5 Write down 3 positive goals, that will impact your life, just do it.
6 Just do it.

**<u>A winner's mentality fuelled by action</u>:** "The best way to predict the future is to invent it." -**Alan Kay.**

No matter how many times you fall down in your life it matters how you rise up and get back up again you are the winner.

## • Thank you Mr Dawson wishing & hoping.

I always thought wishing and hoping was always a part of fairytale dreams and in fantasy books there will always be a place in our world for us as humans to have our moments of wishing.

**"Did you know Cinderella, Snow White, Sleeping Beauty wished and hoped for things to happen but it all didn't happen instantly, no they all had to make a change, work hard and overcome major stumbling blocks before they could live happily ever after?"**

have you heard people say hey im going to make a wish, and wish my life away; "do you really want to wish your life away"? What does your future wish look like if you haven't started on it yet? If you do nothing but wish, nothing will change. 1 year from now is going to come, whether you do nothing or start taking action. The only difference will be the painted blurred picture .My old teacher Mr Dawson once said to me, Wishing and hoping aint strategies for success, but action is

The years I was at Melville high, we had great teacher mentors Kevin Bradley NZ Hammer thrower, Lyn Parker silver fern Netballer, Harry Mahon NZ rowing coach, and of course school teacher Mr. Sam Dawson who I want to acknowledge, was to help me dream, wish and hope with the passion, and to never give up to achieve success

Mr Sam Dawson was well known by all the students of the school and talked about more so, about his hair piece above his head than his physical education and mentoring skills, it happened to be Mr. Dawson would transform me, influence my attitude and personality forever

We had school athletics day , I tried my hand at most events sprinting ,high jump, discus ,long jump ,I was quite good at most of them , but there was one event that I liked the most of all, that was the javelin , I loved throwing things like a cricket ball ,and this thing called a javelin was shaped like a spear, nice and pointy, something you would see on the movie Zulu warrior.

# Thank you Mr Dawson wishing & hoping.

This one event I loved and was so passionate about, I had been blessed with natural ability of having a very strong right arm

All the senior boys were bigger and older than me, but what I had was the technique to throw the javelin further than anyone else

The javelin really excited me for some reason and Mr. Dawson took a likening to me. he came to see me ,and he said WALDEN do you want to go further and represent your school at the interschool zone championships, you have the talent, but have you got what it takes, work hard , commitment & action to go with your talent , if not, I can't help you

if you want to do well. You have 2 choices, 1 you can wish for some time to happen, 2 you can hope and make something happen, you see; our sports team's achievements were quite outstanding on a national scale. Mr Dawson mentioned the words to me again, wishing and hoping, what they mean to you WALDEN; I said I wish I could be the best I can be with the javelin and hope for a better performance. Mr Dawson said the big difference is

**"If you wish for something it may never happen, if you really wish for something you need to take action" Sam Dawson PE Melville High**

The problem with wishing is that you are spending all your time wishing, doing nothing, but never actually doing anything to make it happen, as for Hoping, on the other hand,

Having a desire with real commitment and outcome, a plan with a purpose ,to believe that there is a real possibility ,if you put in the training time , great things can and will happen, believing they can happen ,because you action. That day Mr. Dawson and I went to work on the wishes and hope list, formulating a plan of action to succeed for tomorrow and future, he mention the tomorrow and future words a lot, I remember what he had spoken to me about, and those word about wishing and hoping and they touched my heart to this very day, don't action your wish

# Thank you Mr Dawson wishing & hoping.

, you could end up in a fish, if you don't have hope try soap.

I really do thank him for helping me, teaching, mentoring me in those high school years.

And Yes, those wishes came true that year, and hope had certainly won the reality race, I had won the javelin interschool championships, Waikato bay of plenty championships in bare feet how remarkable, and the North Island Secondary title all in the space of one year , Mr Dawson's philosophies' said ,To wish is to hope that something will come true. And to hope is to wish it could be true.

Questions you may ask yourself
1 What are the wishes, I do want to come true?
2 Have I ever wished for something big or small?
Here are 7 powerful keynote Wish and Hope tips

1 I will Hope for something better?
2 Do you wish you had a different career?
3 I will be hoping for good health.
4 DO YOU wish you were trim and fit?
5 I hope to be in a healthy relationship?
6 Do you wish you were wealthy?
7 What do you hope; your life will look like one year from now, five years or even ten years from now?

## A winner's mentality fuelled by thought: "If you keep wishing, but don't take any action, how can you have hope"?

No matter how many times you fall down in your life it matters how you rise up and get back up again you are the winner.

## • Too much dreaming, not enough doing, very little activity isn't a great recipe for success.

I love New Zealand its beauty plus all the lovely scenery, Angela and I took a trip to Auckland's one tree hill , it's one of my favourite places overlooking all of Auckland, we love Auckland city because she is so beautiful and if you look out north, east, west, and south around each point they all have their own character.

Other people may have different point of view about Auckland in general, as for Angela and I and kids there is an attraction, we have to remember everybody is entitled to their opinion

I must admit, I am one of the biggest dreamers around, looking around from the top of one tree hill,

**"It can leave me and my thoughts and emotions and dreams in a timeless and breathless mood, seems like the world right there and then has fallen at your feet and my mind is fuelled with so many endless possibilities" C.D Walden**

People have got their camera s going, taking spectacular pictures of the wonderful views

Do you know, from where I am standing now, I feel the sense of peacefulness? That it, feels like I am the only one on top of the hill just me and my thoughts. Right now I am dreaming of so much potential and opportunity.

For me places like one tree hill, let me relax, dream, and let my creativity run freely

I don't really want to leave one tree hill and you kind of dream and wish the moments that you have in your mind and heart would stay forever in you

Believe me, it like going to a seminar, that you really like or going to, a Stevie wonder or Justin Timberlake concert ,you're excited and you want to stay longer, you just want for the moment to go on forever, and take them both home with you.

## Too much dreaming, not enough doing, very little activity isn't a great recipe for success.

But in reality just think to yourself, how much hard work, Justin and Stevie put in to make the concert a success.

I know I love the trip up to one tree hill with my wife and family, but

**"I also knew it was time to go back down and pound the pavement of reality and take all my dreams and ideas with me".**

What did I take away from dreaming and brain storming while I was up there, I knew I wanted to shift to Auckland, I knew Auckland was full of many opportunities, but I didn't know which one to take, sometimes this can be a hindrance

**"Inflicting ourselves with the pain of overkill and overload with too many dreams and ideas, we tend to do more dreaming and not enough doing, less activity to enhance our dreams to become that reality".**

We can get tied up with so many dreams all at once and it could lead to disaster.

As I have told you so far, if you have been reading some of the stories in some of those chapters it takes 2 things to happen

**1** dream
**2** Actions.

There is a time to stop dreaming and start putting your dream into action too many people say they have a dream, but really they don't.

# Too much dreaming, not enough doing, very little activity isn't a great recipe for success.

Here is 9 keynote Excuses & reasons why.

**1** No dream
**2** No decision
**3** No plan
**4** I will fail
**5** Fears of what people may say
**6** My dream is too big for me to reach
**7** Procrastination and perfection
**8** No courage
**9** All talk no action.

One of the big reasons a person dream will never amount to anything is because they **"NEVER take responsibly, never action or do anything towards their dream"**

Think about this.

Sometimes we can see the end results of our dream outcomes first, but nothing has happened yet,

Example you can dream of the outcome, of what your house may look like finished, but in reality you have to start with the building process and foundations, we must take action and asked a builder for advice and use the right tools to plan and action to build our dream home.

We can all say to ourselves I dream about losing weight and staying healthy, that's is the outcome which is easy to say and visualize, but im still eating junk food and not exercising, you don't take action to pursue and do. You my friends will not see any change and results.

You have a school university assignment to do, you know the outcome of what grade you can achieve, but what happens if you don't take action, you get the big f from your teacher failed.

I am writing this book winners circle of dreams and if I don't carry on with action then the book doesn't get finished and published, as simple as that, game, set, match all over rover.

## Too much dreaming, not enough doing, very little activity isn't a great recipe for success. "Start with action today"

A lot of dreamers dream to much and wish for things to happen and with little action which will lead to your dreams being poisoned like snake, scorpion, you become paralyzed mind, mentally, creativity wise and remain stagnant, try to read the chapter about attitude & butterfly v spiders you will find it very interesting .With every dream with action you string together, you gain in confidence, you are the winner,

Each little step you take, you are the winner. Momentum propels you to move forward faster, you are the winner.

> And if you hang on to the dream long enough the seeds and fruits of you labour will evolve, definitely you have won

**Questions you may yourself**
1 Do I dream too much too little to late
2 Which dream is the most important to me?
3 Have I taken any action yet?

Here are 6 Keynote tips
1 Make a decision.
2 You know what it is you want to pursue, it's about what you do that matters too.
3 Excitement and Enthusiasm will help you gain the momentum you need
4 Get those activities going
5 Write down what it is you would like to achieve with a deadline
6 Eliminate all excuses

**<u>A winner's mentality fuelled by action</u>:** "I can't imagine a person becoming a success person, without action, who doesn't give this one chance in life everything he or she has got" -**Walter Cronkite.**

No matter how many times you fall down in your life it matters how you rise up and get back up again you are the winner.

- **Without navigation and direction it won't happen.**

**A winner's mentality fuelled by action:** "it's not about where we are at, but the direction we are moving" - **Oliver Wendell Homes.**

Are you dreaming about why it is your dream is not happening yet, if you have read the last chapter about dreaming and action currently you are putting the process in place, then you on the right road to success .

For many people they don't know where to start or begin, just end up without direction.

> **"Your dreams need direction and a road map in your life without them it won't happen you will get lost and won't have any idea where you are going".**

Here are some plain and simple true everyday stories relating to some form of direction

**Story 1** One weekend my wife was invited to a woman's conference, she left me with some instructions, make sure you cook tea and tidy up after you, just keep the house clean and tick them off in your journal what you have done .I love cooking which is one of my favourite, not a problem at all.

Over that weekend the kids ended up with a whole lot of clothes that needed doing

Washing was different prospect for me, you see my wife used the washing machine all the time, I don't think I had ever used it at all.

The landlord had just installed this new washing machine and shown Angela how to use this machine, but not me, only because I thought Angela takes care of the washing needs for all the family.

Well the boys said to me dad I need these clothes done , im ,going out tonight with friends , I said yes ,ok little did they know, I didn't know how to work this washing machine.

# Without navigation and direction it won't happen.

This washing machine was called heavy duty Espirit Simpson 550 with couple of buttons and dial gauge.

The last washing machine I used was the flash gentle Annie touch pad which if it broke down, was a lot to fix

The motto of this story is the washing machine even though I didn't know how to use it gave me a sense of peace of mind and direction, to help me in my time of need

I put the clothes in the washing machine and put the washing power in closed the lid and turned the dial around to the start.

9 key directions of the washing machine
1 super wash
2 maxi wash
3 regular wash
4 normal wash
5 spray rinse
6 deep rinse
7 drip dry/drain
8 spin
9 off/finished.
I found out that after 9 function s even a washing machine starts from a starting point and has a direction and functions to achieve the ultimate goal of clean washed clothes. Im glad I leant something about washing machines and how valuable they are, these days you can't live without them.

**Story 2** The bay of plenty has some of the most beautiful beaches, camping rounds /fishing spots and wonderful people New Zealand has to offer

Recently I was working as driver/sales man doing door to door selling, in today's world with any job it has its moments of challenges and good times and high pressure accountability.

What I liked about the job was getting out into the community and seeing the people and new clients.

# Without navigation and direction it won't happen.

My area covered the bay of plenty which was a wide catchment area
I would have to go from Tauranga each morning to either
1 Te puke
2 Whakatane.
3 Opotiki.
4 kauweru
5 Rotorua
6 Murupara
7 Tokoroa.
Even though I had to travel a distance to see existing clients I didn't mind, I knew I was in control of what direction I was heading too

Back in the past I worked for a company I had to use a road map and the journey would take longer I would get so frustrated trying to find the right address.

On this one particular day the boss called me up he said Craig you have got these 60 clients to see, you are in Rotorua for the whole day because you need to catch up with them, I said ok.

Rotorua has a population of 60,000 people I didn't know the area that well.

Even though I had a list with peoples name on it and addresses I still had to find out, where about they resided in Rotorua.

I am so glad the company had just installed a GPS Tom Tom Navigational System in my vehicle.

WOW I thought saves all the hassle I try it, I turned on the navigational system and it read

# Without navigation and direction it won't happen.

<u>Tom-Tom</u>
HOME
Press
1 Maps – 2 Support
3 Route Planner
4 Live Traffic -
Pressed on 1maps and the GPS give me a map reading of Rotorua and where the vehicle is currently

**Pressed 3 Route Planner and GPS gave me a page and said put in address**

So I did, I put the address of the client into reader and then the Tom Tom Gps printed out my vehicle location and also a road map with instructions of how far away the client is in km and what's even so cool is the Tom Tom would actually talk back to me I had a partner companion with me

**"And all I had to do was listening to the directions and follow the map"**

After doing a few of the clients, it seemed so simple and easy to use,

Thank you Gps you made my day

Thanks to the direction and guidance of GPS technology I was to get through my client base. That day I had seen 80% of the clients.

We can learn so much from a washing machine and GPS Tom Tom.

<u>**A winner's mentality fuelled by action**</u>: "it's not about where we are at, but the direction we are moving" - **Oliver Wendell Homes.**

# Without navigation and direction it won't happen.

**Story 3** "Have you ever been to a factory and seen an assembly line in action, it gives you one direction and keeps going forward and not backwards, it knows where it's going and knows what it will produce at the end result"

I worked at fisher and Paykel in Auckland New Zealand and ended up on the assembly line making fridges, I know what I am talking about

So many end users in today's world see, touch, and feel the finished product, that's all they see, trust me I was at the beginning of the assembly line and watched the direction and process transformation of parts become the fridge.

**Story 4** I am a believer we all have our own beliefs, the scriptures in the holy bible give us sense of powerful direction and purpose to pull towards spiritual faith and abide by the creators commandments.

We have our own laws of governments, land and country; they help guide us, with a purpose of direction

## Our own mind

Just like Our own dreams they need direction, or they won't happen, humans have a great navigational system and that's called our mind, we are a powerful and clever race of people, only trouble for most of us **we don't use our mind fully for what it was designed for.**

Most people find it easy to follow the direction of something else, someone else, work for someone else which is great

**"The upside to this is 95% of the human race, can't navigate and find direction and fulfilment for themselves, we are followers of some ones else's dream, but not our own".**

You must plug into your mind, a written plan of goals and direction so you can follow the right path.

# Without navigation and direction it won't happen.

Ask any courier driver who is delivering parcels to their clients, time deadlines is money; fast navigation is the key and so crucial, not delivering on time, could be the difference, between a profit - loss – expense.

Pilots can't fly a plane in overloaded airspace, fog, stormy weather without direction, written instructions and coordinates.

Once you find out who you are, and dream the dream you would like to turn into reality, we should make a plan for it, direction will quickly control your flight path.

Technology today is so powerful, we have cell phones, iPods, androids, 1phones map readers so many gadgets we still in the end have to make a choice about the direction we are heading in
Questions you may ask yourself

1 Where am I currently going in my life?
2 Am I navigating in the right direction?
3 What is my own sense of purpose?
4 I want to do something amazing with my life.
5 How do I find the right direction to get to the destination?
Here are 15 keynote tips to help us find direction in our life?
1 A daily Dream and goal planner
2 Journals
3 Diaries
4 Process planners
5 Technology planning devices Mobile, Smart phone, IPod
6 Compasses
7 Books, CDs, DVD
8 Events and Functions
9 Prayer and belief
10 Our own mind
11 Follow your own dream and not someone else's dream
12 Visit a factory assembly line.
13 You need Road map.
14 GPS Tom Tom. NavMan
15 The bible

# Time for change.

Time for a change, isn't it, you know we are changing every day of our lives regardless, we are all ageing, time will always be, but the key is

> **"What changes are we going to make with the time we have allocated to us here on this earth? If we are to use time in a smart way, the changes that we do make will be of benefit to us"? CD Walden.**

Are you ready for change, that is the big question, get excited, don't be scared of change, If we change our own attitudes we can influence our own lives, Im actually not being sarcastic or anything, I will fill your heart with positive words of encouragement, hopefully by now you are starting to understand yourself, you are gaining momentum and strength, confidence, And are enjoying the book winners circle of dreams and the stories that can relate to you

I got an email from my nephew the other day he said he wanted to talk to me on face book, so I got online, there he was, I said Daniel how are things going this is what he said

April 4$^{th}$ 2013
Uncle Craig, how have you been?
**Daniel,** *how are you doing?*
Uncle Craig, am writing a book at the moment
How is dad
***Daniel I am great at the moment um how is your book coming along??? Um don't know how dad is, think he still in that home um I am living in Brisbane now***

Uncle Craig good on you, wow what are you doing over there, so happy for you

***Daniel just working at the moment as scaffold worker trying to save so I can go visit Paris some day***

Uncle Craig who are you staying with
hey your uncle did Xfactor, anything is possible

# Time for change

So proud of you Daniel, make something for yourself, you can do it

Some people back in New Zealand are doing nothing, but you have made a change, good on you

Got one life make the most of it, don't look back at the past it's the future that's exciting

*Daniel how did you do in Xfactor??? Is Jeremy still on his mission???? I didn't want to be one those people uncle sitting around for the rest of their life's ... you know what I mean ae uncle I changed, hows the rest of the family???*

Yes Jeremy's overseas
**Daniel Seattle ae.**
Alisha is finished her degree in graphics
         Andrews bought his own house in Te Atatu
*Daniel Australia is so cool with so many opportunistic things to do*

*It's better to change than not at all*

*Daniel but ill back in Christmas time come for ae visit after the New Year*

*If that's all right with you uncle...*

I was totally blown away by what Daniel had said to me

1 I thought he was still in Hamilton New Zealand

2 I knew he was a doorman at night club.

3 I didn't think he had it in him to want to get up and go to Brisbane

4 Wow now I realised Daniel had taken the initiative in his life to make a change and take control I love what he said**???? I didn't want to be one those people, uncle sitting around for the rest of their lives ... you know what "I changed to do something better for my life".**

# Time for change

The Daniel I used to know had changed from that young boy, to a young man who was confident and ready to give changes ago.

"Is the opportunity of change knocking at our door?
That answer is "yes" each and every day of our lives

Why, all you have to do is observe and be sensitive to the things you see and what is around you",

There are only two choices in life **to say yes or no**, to what it is we would **like to do**, and **not do** that's how simple life and change is "really".
Just think a message can change ones heart. That's opportunity, a time to reflect to make change.

I was out watching kite boarding and the wind surfers , my wife and I didn't see too many people out and about , was the weather to unkind for others , or was it a change in the weather ,windy and rough waves  choppy , an opportunity and change in  conditions the kite boarding and surfers thrived and took advantage of.

Have you ever been to an event that was irrelevant to you at first? , it started of as a meaningless gesture, then someone at the event said something to you, they wanted to do business with you, and you came back home, had a change of heart and your eyes opened up to opportunity, I'm so glad I went to that event after all, I would never have been given the opportunity

Dreams opportunity and change could come knocking at your door today, it could be at Events and places we lest expect. How many events have you missed, instead of being filled with rave reviews are filled with regret?

Events family ,church ,sporting events, business events , even your children's prize giving event is so special in recognition of change and what he ,or she has done, they are so important in our lives

1 Don't miss family events.
2 Don't miss the work meeting.
3 Don't miss church Sunday.
4 Don't miss your Child's sports day and prize giving.
5 Don't miss the wedding anniversary.
6 Don't miss the meeting with your client.

# Time for change

They are so important in our lives.
**Please go, or you just might miss change and opportunity, you may never get another chance.**

My sister in-law carol and her partner decided to make a change in their lives  are currently travelling Europe and doing the great OE Overseas experience  they are more excited about going to different continents and seeing and learning about amazing cultures.

My son Andrew and his partner have just bought their first home at 21yrs of age what an amazing life change for them.

Our other son is on a mission in the Marshall Islands between Guam and Hawaii and changed his lifestyle and sacrificed his job and his social life to serve to others who are less fortunate.
Our daughter Alisha and Jessie lives have changed, have acquired new jobs in Auckland, the list of change will continue to evolve and grow

Both my wife and I have experienced change within our family in so many ways as most other parents do.

We watch our babies from birth change and develop into young kids; through to teens young adults and change again finally take a step out into the big wide world.

**A winner's mentality fuelled by action:** "Change is said to be the miracle and cure to life, change takes transformation every single day of our lives".

when you dream a big dream, you want to change to follow that dream, today is today and tomorrow, one week from now 1 year 5 years 20 years from now, you would have changed, changes and events move from one extreme to another, sadness to happiness, defeat to conquer, loser to winner, hate to love, life and death, season to season winter, summer, spring, fall.

Are we ready to change for ourselves personally to be the best, only we have the answer, You can be sure if you make Change today .you will benefactor /sowing the change and reaping a winning harvest.

# Time for change

**Questions to ask yourself**
1 What can I do to change?
2 Can I change my way of thinking?
3 I want to change my old habits?
4 My attitudes got to change from negative to positive?

Here are 9 keynote life changing tips, do it today.


**1** Get a new makeover Maybe is about time we look at what we really see in the mirror ,Your image of what you see right now, might be the one thing you feel is holding you back and making you lack confidence.

If you've had the same old tired look for ages, then it may be time to change transform your appearance in so many ways. spend a couple of $$$ on yourself, you will feel better about you, do it get that new makeover, hairstyle, you have always wanted, lose that weight, buy the new wardrobe shoes, clothes, jewellery, just do those things to make you feel so special. You will feel like a million bucks, amazing, comfortable, and confident, positive so excited, your whole personality will move up another level, make change today just do it.

**2** Hey if the job is just not for me, do it change, I will give you 2 choices, toss it, dwell in it , you will know, you have changed when you know what it is you really want to do, The only thing preventing you finding something that you'll enjoy more, is you, its better to change and love what you do, than to be stuck with something you hate doing ,make a change today do it, see a coach or recruitment work consultant ,im sure there won't be a problem.

**3** Never ever travelled before, try the travel bug, do it make a change, I ask my sister in law how she is enjoying the travel she said she loves it, travel the world, because the world is waiting for

# Time for change

you, just imagine that backpacking trip around the globe, then consider going to some far away location where the culture experience will be totally different — perhaps even life-changing. Make a change today do it get on the phone talk to your travel agent about your dream plans.

**4** Buying your first dream house. You may want to buy your first home like my son and his partner did do it, change. Make a change today, do it start saving, go for a drive, look at houses in your area that are for sale that you might like

**5** Do charity work and serve others
Charity work makes us feel good about ourselves while we do something practical to help others. I honestly believe it is an act of kindness from your heart. Charity work also inevitably means having greater opportunities to meet other people. There are plenty of charitable organisations that would be open to you helping out; I gave up my time by simply giving up a few hours a week to help a young man with disabilities to do his shopping. I found it to be so life changing realising there are people out there that are less fortunate than you, while you do your charity work, it will have a profound and lasting effect on people you help.

**6** Activate and get fit
I got my running shoes on and love walking, and its free, have you?, if u are sick of slumping in front of the TV and gaming devices after coming home from work maybe it's time to change. try walking or joining the gym or zumbia dance group , some people like working by themselves, others will need to find a trainer to help them inspire to get results, if you will take some action today  then it's likely you'll start feeling a lot healthier in a short space of time. Make a change today do it run around the lake smell the fresh air ,good for your mind ,call the gym ask for a trainer he can help you with your transformation of change to live longer.

# Time for change

**7** Change your diet
I like to feel great don't you? ,go take a look in the mirror , what you see is what you got, 'You are what you eat' is a much-used phrase, and it may be that your diet is making you feel so sick . By just changing what you put into your mouth the good foods and fluids can have positive health benefits as well as give you more energy and make you feel better all round. My wife's mums Edwina says eat everything in moderation; it is the best way to go. I love her cooking. Make sure you drink enough water and get your five portions of fruit and veg; they are two of the best golden rules to follow. Make a change today, I found some healthy recipes' online; I say stay healthy and wealthy to live longer, what's the use of having a lot of wealth when you are unhealthy and possibly have a shortened life.

**8** Everyone is capable of doing something special in their life, are you? If not," pinch yourself", make a change? Make the most of doing that something special

**9** If you are finding things are getting tough and at a crossroad in life I am a believer, but shouldn't we all believe in something.

**A winner's mentality Fuelled by action:** "What we can do is "prey" and you will receive that revelation of change"- **The Apostle Jesus Christ.**

No matter how many times you fall down in your life it matters how you rise up and get back up again you are the winner

# CHAPTER 4 NOTES

# Chapter 5

## • Write down your dreams today, you can see your future

"One way to gain momentum is to see where our target is, so we can quickly get there, but you must write down your dreams and goals with purpose and action" today and not tomorrow.

I have given you some key tips about how to change, maybe you know already or have got something better in mind, and that's ok .but don't let your mind-set pursued you, to not give whatever it is a go, what we tend to do, is not write our dreams or goals down, we can't see them on paper on the fridge or in a journal so we go blind and cannot measure how we are going with our performances. Whether it is making an appointment, with your bank manager, having a baby, running a marathon, climbing the highest mountains, losing weight, new makeup, buying a pet, saving up for that new car or that house or trip around the world, or alternatively wanting to change jobs for some career ambition, have them written down on paper somewhere, If you don't see any momentum going forward in your life, then you can quickly become dishearten. **establishing a plan with action, a target with a time line will help you work towards gaining momentum changing and achieving and getting all the things you want in life,** you will get motivated and keep focused stay on track, it also helps prevent you from just drifting along and falling into a rut — so remember with every dream or goal you wish to pursue with momentum, is the difference between the winners and the losers?

**"Starting writing down your dreams and goals today not tomorrow, what are you waiting for, start writing and you will see your future unfold".** If we are to achieve anything great in life with our dream and take it to the next level .we must commit and take the first step to writing them down and I do agree whole heartily with that statement, it will make the journey so easy for us to see where we are heading, if we have a process performance plan so we can take

# Write down your dreams today, you can see your future

the necessary action to achieve what we want to achieve, its as simple as that

I firmly believe when you write things on paper in your journal, iphone, calendar chances are, you will get the dream goal task done.

Writing down the dream goal and task, with a timeline sets major events in motion in your life.

If you didn't make a start with writing something down on paper, then no events, achievements or success, would not be possible otherwise.

The book Winners circle of dreams started out just as thought in my mind, I knew I had the eagerness, reason and passion to go ahead and write down all the things I needed to do to publish my book, and to do motivational speaking The starting point its all up to me, the bucks starts with me, achievement is eagerness and ambition. I keep this constantly in my mind.

**"Big dreams big results Weak dreams bring weak results, a small fire makes a small amount of heat." So, your first step in goal setting and achieving your dreams is that you've got to light a big fire in your heart so no one can put the flames out",**

Everyone will see you mean business that you are prepared to achieve the dream, you are brighter than light house \*\*\*

I went shopping the other day to get groceries, my wife Angela and I, talked about what we needed to get, she said Craig you better write it down, you could come back with things you don't need or you might forget some things you do need. If you can do you're shopping and write a list down and follow the list and bring them back.

**"Same principle applies, written dreams and goals are the same as the shopping list, you know what it is you want, you just have to go out and get it and pick them up".**

# Write down your dreams today, you can see your future

One other great thing about writing your dreams and goals down on paper is you will start to feel good about yourself ,your whole personality will change, get so excited, Those times ,I know that when I do something I love doing ,and I know what is it, and can see it clearly happening in my life, and I have achieved a milestone , it does so much to me, so many people have written goals and dreams down have experienced joy and happiness and success as an end result . So get going start writing down today not tomorrow decide with passion, what is it is you would like to do? writing down your dreams today is the best thing you can do, and you will have no regrets doing it, you will have  mapped out your future in front of you, you are on the your journey of success, and you will become a part of  the winners circle of dreams

Questions to ask yourself

1 Where is my target I can see

2 What's my target?

3 When was the last time I wrote my dreams and goals down on a piece of paper?

Here are 5 keynote tips to help with your future

1 Dreams and goals written down on paper show the future.

2 Don't wait, and put off for tomorrow, right them down.

3 Why not start today.

4 You need to get excited; you will feel better seeing those dreams and goal written down.

5 A written set of dreams and goals a like a shopping list, all I have to do is go out and pick them up.

**A winner's mentality fuelled by action** "Your destiny is not a matter of chance but a matter of planned choices waiting to be achieved" - **William Jennings Bryan**

No matter how many times you fall down in your life it matters how you rise up and get back up again you are the winner.

- **Voyager of the seas dream cruise, taking a photo just doesn't cut.**

Merry Christmas and Happy New Year 2012 /2013 and how are the resolutions going, I hope you got everything you wished for over the Christmas period and Santa has treated you most kindly, and currently you are full steam ahead heading towards your resolutions 2013

My wife and spent our first day of 2013 at one of the beach hot spots of Mount Maunganui in NZ, it was such a beautiful and wonderful day ,one of the driest summers New Zealand has experienced over the last 15 yrs. .

The weather was so magnificent there where so many people out enjoying the sun surf and beach.

Every summer season the Mount Maunganui population increases between Christmas and New Year's aligned with holiday makers from everywhere all over New Zealand and abroad.

There has been also an increase in cruise ships visiting the port of Tauranga.

My wife had dragged me off the couch after we had New Year's lunch and said, it's too good to be inside, the weathers great, we need to go for a, walk and burn off all your calories so you can stay in shape.

So I did, what I was asked to do, and we ended up going for a walk around the mount.

Why did we really come out of our house to be among the crowd? I ask myself, well turns out my wife told me, as we were driving in the car, she wanted to go and see a ship her friends were talking about, and I said, a ship, "what for"? , it's only a boat, man; I could be home watching sports on the TV.

## Voyager of the seas dream cruise, taking a photo just doesn't cut.

As we drove closer to the port we could see a glimpse of the boat as I got closer and closer to pilot bay wharf off Mount Maunganui I realized this boat wasn't just a boat, but a super cruise liner, one of the world's biggest super cruise ships

There she stood so grand her Name, Voyager of the Seas, the cruise liner was in port for just whole day and due to leave at 6pm that evening. New Year's afternoon, going around the mount, was not so bad after all, we saw runners going up and around the mount, mums and dad pushing their babies around and families relaxing eating ice-cream

As we were walking around the base of Mount Maunganui we made a stop to talk with some of the people from off the voyager of the seas, who were taking photos of some of the great scenery the mount had to offer, most of the passengers were from the USA and doing a South Pacific cruise down under, which would take in other parts of New Zealand, Australia, and Pacific island

The couple we spoke to said they had been on the Voyager of the seas over the last 38 days they said New Zealand has been one of their favourite stop off spots, you kiwis are so friendly, and it is so peaceful here in New Zealand.

# Voyager of the seas dream cruise, taking a photo just doesn't cut.

## 3% v.i.p club of success.

That day I had to ask the couple, what's it like on the boat?

How they described it to us, my wife and I tried to imagine what it was like. The couple called it the floating hotel due to the amazing facilities; they said **we were treated like 1$^{st}$ class royalty.** They gave my wife and I some information about the boat, an insight to what it was like to take a cruise and why, definitely we were sold their on their dream

On board this magnificent super cruiser are 3150 guests, one of the largest passenger ships in the world. The ship measures 137,276 gross tons with a displacement of 64,000 tons. It is 1,020 ft. long overall, has a waterline beam of 127 ft. and a maximum width of 156 ft (47.55 m).

**Voyager of the seas features.**
1 The world's first rock climbing wall.
2 An ice staking ring
3 A marble floored street stretching just over ¾ the length of the ship and features
FOUR shops and light dining venues.
4 Three-story main dining room
Restaurants
5 Themed bars and lounges
6 Day Spar and Fitness Centre
7 Wedding chapel
8 Swimming Pools
9 Library Teen Club
10 "The Vault" Nightclub
15 decks high
11 10 whirl pools & pools
12 14 bars clubs & lounges.

# Voyager of the seas dream cruise, taking a photo just doesn't cut.

My wife and I were impressed with what we had heard from the couple from of the ship "who wouldn't be" I just had to ask one cheeky question, "does it take lot of money to go on a cruise" "do you have to be super wealthy", they replied for some, it's not so much about the money that interest us,

**"It's all about the dream and life style and experience, why, how, when to take action, timing, thrill and journey, we planned our dream",**

To others it may be a lot of money, instantly if you have to pay straight away

If you dream, plan, it's worth doing and waiting for.

# Voyager of the seas dream cruise, taking a photo just doesn't cut.

## • 97% holiday club ticket to almost someday.

That evening a crowd of 5,000 followers aligned with their cameras, iphone, technical devices clicking and snapping away on the banks of pilot bay, anyone would of thought the paparazzi had arrived, to grab some big headline story, there was no deigning voyager of the seas was equal to pop star liked status, watched the movie titanic the scene where titanic is about depart, people everywhere, the atmosphere is electric and jack Dawson

And his friend had just collected their winning from a poker game and a won ticket in that process that changed their lives forever to go on the titanic and how excited they were.

That evening at 6pm the voyager of the seas started to take off, we heard some of the followers in the background mention these things

**1** We can't afford it we got photos anyway.
**2** Rich wealthy buggers
**3** Why can't we go on the boat
**4** You have to be a millionaire to go on that ship.
**5** They are lucky.
**6** We are too busy to go on that ship.
Sometimes we are our own worst critics, we get caught up in the hype of a moment we decide, **1** we are going to make a resolution, **2** Family we going to go on that ship, but we never do, We can take as many photos as we like, to show our friends and family or use face book and put them on the bath room door, the only problem is we will never experience, what it will be like to go on a super cruise ship like the voyager of the seas.

# Voyager of the seas dream cruise, taking a photo just doesn't cut

**"Hey we all can say it felt like we were almost there, but yet so far away".**

but yet as followers right now ,we can only see from the outside but if do something today, we book a ticket today, ring the travel agent and take action, we can really get to know what voyager of the seas has to offer from the inside . If you don't do anything, the ticket you receive is the trip to someday that leads to a place called nowhere

Ever bought GYM equipment accessories from a 0800 ad if you purchased it, why is it gathering dust, you will not get fit if you leave your equipment locked away in the closet and you are not using it.

What was the purpose of buying the equipment in the first place? Same thing

A couple approached us Michael and Katie they were real-estate agents from a major company.

They heard us talking about people and their comments.

I said wow look at all these people taking photos, how many of these 5000 followers will want to go on a trip ,but what are they doing about it .Michael turned around , said to me ,are you a speaker or something? I said I am writing a book called winners circle of dreams, he said what's it all about, I said it's about the winning in you.

**And are you speaking soon? I said very soon**

Michael said how much do you charge? I said I will come back to you soon,

I have 300 hundred staff, which needs to find that reason, you have been talking about Craig, and this year in 2013 they need to get fired up and produce goals and set targets.

# Voyager of the seas dream cruise, taking a photo just doesn't cut

Would you come and talk to them, Angela my wife looked at me she was over the moon, I was in demand and my business had not started yet, so amazing.

Michael and Katie ask me, what the secret is.? I said, what the couple, I met up with, had said to me, is so true, take a look at yourself first, got to dream big, and find the reason why, how and action do it, and there lies the answer

If any of your staff want to be successful, they have to find a reason.

why do you want to sell more houses, maybe setting a goal to go on the cruise with family is a great start, it will help speed up the process of selling the house ,and increase their sales.

If someone says im selling houses for a living, selling houses is the vehicle, but not the reason.

I talk with Mike and Katie about commitment, if you can commit to a marriage it's a business, if you can commit to something like a marriage, you will succeed. Later on in this book I will talk about commitment and marriage how they both intertwine with each other

> **"Remember we need that dream, reason, why, how, when to succeed**
>
> **Too many people stop trying and give up and have no dream and not a big enough reason with heart"**

# Voyager of the seas dream cruise, taking a photo just doesn't cut.

## Look there's a price to pay to dream.

Remember the couple we talk to, they gave us some advice, here is what they said, there is a price to pay, with anything you do, we have a reason, it wasn't so much about the money, we got plenty money saved, Where ever you are, at this time in your life, it's something we learn and should all draw on. Seriously we all can learn a thing or too

**"I am here for the dream, journey, lifestyle, and an experience, and time is so short, with a photo, you can capture the moment, but go experience a dream, journey, lifestyle, and it stays with you forever"**

So with Each new life style experience we have today, tomorrow, future, take it on the run, that becomes a new part of what we are, and who we can be.

People think just because you have a ton of money you are happy, for some that happens, we are retired, time to us is so valuable, it what you do with your money that matters. You got to do something

We are just a lot like you, got so excited, when the ships come in to port, taking photos, we come from Southern California in the USA and I would take a photo of the front of the boat and when they left port I would take photos of the back of the boat, I was so sad and curious, I could not take photos of what was between both front and the back of the boat.

Then one day I decided to put my photos up in my house, my wife and I started dreaming and found a reason, why, what would it be like to go on a journey of a life time and take a cruise down under to the south pacific, we took action ready for a life changing and eventful experience and Booked our tickets.

# Voyager of the seas dream cruise, taking a photo just doesn't cut.

So here we are today enjoying the fruits of our dream to sail the seas,

Guess what the middle of the boat is so impressive we are taking so many photos

> **A winner's mentality fuelled by action:** "**Time** is so valuable in our life, we weren't going to wait around for people to make up our minds for us again, it was never about having lots of money to do the things you want, it was all about the dream, and reason, you wish to pursue, we are the winners, in the end that's all that matters". **Californian Couple 2012**

No matter how many times you fall down in your life it matters how you rise up and get back up again you are the winner.

# CHAPTER 5 NOTES

# Chapter 6

# *How to Work out, what you're top dream is.

So you don't know what your dream is yet?, don't do anything crazy, remember there are lots of people in the same boat as you, here is the truth about why it's taken you so long to decide, you always had a dream, many people have used the no word, so many times, have said you can't do that, it's impossible.

**"Don't worry, people will not protect you from failures, when I think about all of the knock backs, setbacks, I have had, it's time to make that comes back" C D Walden**

My top dream at this time is to finish this book winners circle of dreams , which I am so passionate about, if I want this so bad I will do anything do make sure of the outcome, I am so sure you can get what you want too. To stay so focused on the dream is very important to your success, and with small commitments to achieve and more hard work to process and grind out; I can't wait to cross the finish line.

Look Don't wait for others to decide, what your top dream is, im sure the last couple in the last chapter about going on a cruise trip didn't wait around for someone to say hey you have my permission to travel, the old couple activated the dream and did it, start giving yourself permission first, to prepare for the start of your race, so sooner you front up at the start line you will feel good, have you ever had to make a quick decision on the spot it's a similar feeling that comes into play or risk doing something unusual, or have you heard someone say I've got a gut feeling, that's call trust in your instincts.

I have had different jobs all of my life at 52 I didn't know, I would be writing a book or doing motivational speaking ,you see life is rather funny at times, with all the things I have done so far have contributed to ,events, life experience and that great

Don't expect to be able to work out what your top dream is overnight "yet", but you'll get there.

# How to Work out, what you're top dream is.

It's taken me time, to find out whom I really am, that's my point, "find out who you really are", and "who you really want to be", true happiness lies directly "in front of you".

You probably know what your dream is already; remember the time is now to trust your instincts, our instincts are usually right.

I wanted to know, how to go about finding out what my dreams were so I started to do a bit of soul searching with myself, this is what I did ,I started to ask myself questions and I got a pen and paper and wrote them down and was amazed with what I came up with ,it didn't fix my problems overnight but it really challenged me to take a good look at myself , saying if I make conscious decision to devote a weekend, put sometime aside away from everybody else ,go somewhere ,find a retreat a hideaway, get lost where no one can find me ,I will discover myself, I'm sure I would know what my top dreams are. Here is what I came up with

<u>3 Quick tips</u>
**1** Grab pen and paper.
**2** Go somewhere away from everyone.
**3** Start brainstorming ideas and dreams and goals.

Questions to ask you're self.

**1** How were my childhood days teenage years and adult years
**2** what did I enjoy doing, what was my favourite toy, sport, book and place.
**3** What made me totally happy?
**4** What did I love doing at school and home?
**5** How is life treating me now?

**6** What have I learnt from my past?
**7** How do I feel?

# How to Work out, what you're top dream is.

## SO I started to write it all down.

I was starting to imagine what my future was like, what I could do in 6 months' time and 2 yrs. time what would life be really like.

I discovered what my priorities were, where do they lie now? I even look back at my past childhood, through to now, what's stopping me from achieving my dreams, what's holding me back, along with all the excuses and negativity and fears

I realized in some areas ,I had sold myself short , I wasn't happy with me ,I had listen to others and their opinions, and not mine, how stupid of me ,so with no time to waste , change was the key, I needed an overhaul immediately.

Then and there I started to eliminate impossible, to what was possible, my mind set changed quickly

**"I started to think good thoughts, and concentrate on the things that I loved doing and things that made me happy",**

I started to pursue them. I started to go walking and do positive things and got a new makeover and to feel better about myself, I was on the way out of darkness and into the light and once I knew I had found that dream I started to prepare myself for the starting line.

# How to Work out, what you're top dream is.

Here are 10 keynote tips to help you and give you an idea what your top dream could look like.

**1** <u>Write a list all the things</u> that make you happy, all the things that you'd like to do, if you are to achieve any dream or planning on pursuing a top dream .Be happy and positive, if you are not happy with what you are doing now, there is always time to change, Focus on happiest times of your life, what you were doing, who you were doing it with, and where you were doing it

**2** <u>Everyone's loves doing something</u> that is why we all have our own special hobby

A Try going back to your past
B What were your hobbies then?
C Move forward to the present.
D Now do you like comic books, gaming on your blog, computer, software, writing poetry, cooking, make up and beauty, it's very possible that these are your passions.

Those hobbies need some serious thought, think about whether they're things you love to do, you might think of starting your own business, do it for a living.

**3** <u>We all have Got the Xfactor</u> ,what hidden Xfactor talent have you got  It's been said that we each have at least one gift we've been given, and that the true purpose of our lives is discovering that gift, and sharing it with the world. There is much truth in that statement, what are you good at

**4** <u>If a genie granted you 3 wishes</u> and 1 of them was a dream job, what you would pick, find out who you would like to work for, who you are working with. You should enjoy a very good working environment and the team of people you work with.

**5** <u>Did you know the work industry and opportunities are there waiting for you.</u>

# How to Work out, what you're top dream is.

Do you see yourself as a trainer, teacher that's a clue to your dream job?

If you love retail and sales people, or clothes, self-employed, that's a clue. If you like singer/song writing or playing the guitar, you are about to discover your passion and dream. If you see yourself as an accountant, author, speaker, model, actor, in a classroom, on construction site, Army, Navy seal, where you work is also an important factor in your dream ,you may want to ask others about the job they are currently doing ,and what is it about the job that makes them happy.

6 <u>You want to be successful ,get passionate and excited about your dream</u>

If you know of someone who has the same dream as you, find out why they are so passionate and what excites them, about what it is they do, find out how other people are living their dream. I write to my mentors all the time, I contact them on face book. They help me Find out what steps they took to get there, what's required, and how they did it.

Get passionate about something you love to do while you're taking your steps to realizing your dream, practice your passion. The more you practice passion the more you believe, you will want to be as good as you can be.

7 Clarity of vision for a big dream.

**Do you know top leaders top companies top coaches and sports people have clear vision ,for many it was the key, to successfully unlocking, achieving their dreams, once they discovered it. Today take time out to picture and visualize , exactly what your dream is, what your dream would be like, how you see yourself doing it, what you're surrounded by, who you're working with.**

# How to Work out, what you're top dream is.

8 <u>You need direction and a road map</u>; sometimes there is more than one road or path to go down to get to a destination. Write down on paper a bunch of ideas for getting there, activation, activity, actions you can take to move yourself closer to your destination. Then put them together into your roadmap.

9 <u>Sense of Purpose and inspiration, please, put aside any other goals for now and focus on the big one</u>

Right now I am focused on my big dream the book the winners circle of dreams published completely and their aint no other dream that takes its place, I give this dream top priority and the other dreams have to wait their turn,. That means you need to put aside any other goals for now, I have one purpose in life. Focus and simplify my life so that I can keep focus on that one big dream.

I use a mission statement and put it on the fridge in writing, if it's to be it's up to me, I look at it and say it several times a day.

# How to Work out, what you're top dream is.

You have to get inspired find others who are trying to achieve the same dream, I Put up pictures from magazines to inspire me. Read motivational books. If I get inspired, I will have the energy needed to get there.

You have to seek motivation; motivation will keep you on your path. Motivation and focus are the keys to achieving any goal.

Making a church commitment, writing in my journal, sticking to timeframes, inspiring others, tracking my progress, stay healthy.

**10 Time**

As they say life is about a place & journey. Time is critical, time will wait for no one, and you will not get anywhere if you don't put the time into your dream. Use your time clock each day for working towards your dream. The Consistent small steps you take, is better doing than none all, and will lead you closer to you dream .

Set aside time either in the morning, or in the evening, or some time when you know you will do it every day. Make it a habit, and you will succeed.

**A winner's mentality fuelled by action:**" Every great dream begins with a dream. Always remember, you have within you the strength, the patience, and the passion to reach for the stars to change the world." **-Harriet Tubman**

No matter how many times you fall down in your life it matters how you rise up and get back up again you are the winner.

- **Visualize your dreams and use affirmation.**

I have great news for you, there is a way to achieve your dreams and goals you must have enough motivation and discipline hard work and sustained action to keep perusing them until you reach them. Because most goals can't be reached overnight, a key component is to use visualization

**"Even a woman has to wait for nine months before she is holding the actual baby in her hand, what does she do, she gets all excited paints a picture and visualizes what the baby's going to look like, feel like"**

Most people lose motivation along the way as a result, I want it to happen now, im to impatient, I don't believe, I don't have a plan, I will, I will not or im not disciplined can't wait, my dream is to far away and is impossible .

Now if you managed to visualize your goals and dreams every day you will make sure that you are always motivated to peruse them and as a result your chance of reaching your big dream will become reality. They are achievable, and believable

Recently my wife and I tried going to a show home , people say why are you doing that, it cost money, who says you can't dream **it's called visualizing for your future home,** besides dreams are free , its only when you are ready to pursue them the hard work starts  we tried it, go and see the house you will love it, move around in the house, see how each room looks like, touch some of the furniture and see how it feels like to sit on a certain lounge suit .**The more you see, touch and feel your dream, is the more passionate you will become about it** .I not only have my future house picture on the fridge, I have my other dreams and goals scattered around the place, and I see them clearly every day,

When a person can see their dreams everyday like me, it reminds me of my obligations and my commitment I have to myself, and to my family, so I will do whatever it takes to make the future happen.

# Visualize your dreams and use affirmation.

when was the last time you went to your local car dealer, but you haven't got the money right now, how are you going to know it in details, if you never seen the car from the inside? You can search the internet for pictures of the car put them on the garage door or in the bathroom in the toilet where ever you can see them, or even better you can go to the dealer, and sit inside the car or even take a test drive in order to know how exactly it feels like to drive it. Go one step further order the car you want, pay for it, and take it, as simple as that. The dreams will be fuelled with emotions you manage to stimulate while visualizing your dream

Since I have been writing this book, I take a look at my diary or look on the fridge at my dreams and goals, I call it repetition, I have to look at my dreams and goals because

**"The more you visualize your performance and dreams the more will your mind power engrains them and the more likely will they turn into reality, and you are at peace, you can believe and feel and touch, your big dream is close to you".**

Another example is each day without delay, I use little inserts from my book winners circle of dreams, although at this time it is not published, and it will be published, I keep blogging on face book to keep that dream very real and alive.

If you are in a situation where your dream is about to die, it can be rekindled, again don't underestimate the power of visualization, for it can do wonders in ones person's life.

**I talk about "Comedian Jim Cary recently in my book and his struggle with success, and how he was broke, before he become famous and the fake check he had in his wallet he wrote to himself, he was faking it, before he made it and he used visualization, and believed he was a star without having a contract signed. In the end Jim Cary won".**

## Visualize your dreams and use affirmation.

Many professional sports codes use video and repetition review the best plays in the games, Olympic sports stars who use picture and visualization in the area of sport at the last Olympic games, my wife and I **watched the heavy weight competitions we were quite amazed at how much these weight lifters could lift with a picture in their mind and the power of visualization they could lift 20kg more than their body weight, they had already pictured and projected a wining lift in their minds.**

**A winner's mentality fuelled by action:** "he who can call himself a leader, has the vision and conviction, that a dream can be achieved, he inspired the power & energy to get things done" - **Ralph Lauren**

No matter how many times you fall down in your life it matters how you rise up and get back up again you are the winner.

## • Dream to stay in the game long enough to win.

Since 2008 I had been following a particular secondary's schools rugby team here in New Zealand, In 2012 at that time I was also writing rugby college articles in conjunction with TV, it gave me a close insight on the who, what, how, why, this school was so successful, it was also taking me on a new fresh adventure in my life, I should tell you, I am a fanatic of most sport. The team I am about to mention in this chapter, had a wonderful rugby pedigree, They had played 23 games win 21 loss 2 record reached the semi-final top 4 $1^{st}$ XV schools in the country 2012

I closely, was following their progress and thought, what has been their secret to success this year; they had won most of their games and reached the knockout stages of the national competition in New Zealand. Here you have it the proof is in the pudding as they say, the Rugby$1^{st}$ xv had built up a very impressive record over the past 7 years and since that time reached the finals 5 times and won 2 national championships .since 2005 have only lost 3 games of rugby at their home ground to date Hamilton BHS: 2003-2013

Played: 214
Won: 179
Lost: 33
Drawn:
For: 6792
Against: 2093
Average Score: 32-10

Major Honours

Super Eight Champions: 2006, 2007, 2008, 2009, 2010, 2012, 2013

National Top Four Winners: 2008 (Unbeaten), 2009 2013

# Dream to stay in the game long enough to win.

Moascar Cup Holders: 2008-2010, 2013 (17 defences, Outscored Their opponents 441-159)

Sannix World Youth Champions: 2010, 2011 (Scored 607 points in 12 games)

Chiefs Cup Champions: 2012 / 2013

## I emailed to the coach and congratulated him, it had been a long season

2012

Hi Greg, just lending my support for your management team and the 1st xv, and I know they have had a great season so far and deserve all the accolades.

I have been monitoring their progress, and have seen some of their games in 2012. It also has been a privilege to watch some of the other young talent 1st xv teams from around the country and on TV.

So you and your team have come this far ,how exciting that is, not only for the school, but for the parent, and the avid fans like me , and old boys of the school, in general, making the Waikato proud .

### *Wish you all the best with the knock-out campaign against, Rotorua - Wesley*

Cheers
Craig Walden.

# Dream to stay in the game long enough to win.

A friend asks me the other day, why is Hamilton boys high so good? why are they one of the best rugby schools in the country?, he said, "are they very lucky"?, and I said, mate it's not about luck, it's all about hard work, I said ,we can all sit on the side line and be critics, but it won't change any bearing on a outcome of the game.

You have to get into game and be ready to stay and endure long enough to know how it's going to play out.

In 2012 Hamilton Boys High were knocked out by Auckland St Kentigern College 29- 13 in the semi-final of the national 1$^{st}$ xv rugby comp, Hamilton had come so close to topping of a great season and gaining another national championship and yet so far, it wasn't meant to be.

IN 2013 just half of the 2012 team had returned for another rugby season ,with experience and lessons learnt from 2012, Hamilton lost their first pre-season game to Kings College of Auckland at home in 2013. The loss would be their first and last for the 2013 season, in the semi-finals of the 2013 national 1$^{st}$ xv at Rotorua , Hamilton beat Wellington College, St Kentigern beat Otago Boys High, So to the final of the National 1$^{st}$ xv for 2013 both Hamilton and St Kentigern from Auckland meet once again in a final and face off, for a second time in 2yrs, last year's 2012 National final was played at Auckland at the home of St Kentigern which they won, this year's 2013 final will be at Hamilton, which would be an intriguing and talked about game and history in the making for 1$^{st}$ xv rugby, Hamilton had a wonderful season winning the chiefs cup, Moascar cup, Super 8 for the 7$^{th}$ consecutive time, St Kentigern college had an amazing record of 52 wins on the trot, stemming from 2011, made the final of the national 1$^{st}$ xv rugby comp, and won the Sanix World Youth 1XV championship, one again were firm favourites, in 2013 Hamilton reversed the defeat of 2012 to beat St Kentigern 12 -10.

**A winner's mentality fuelled by action:** "The strength of the team is each individual member. The strength of each member is the team." - **Phil Jackson**

# Dream to stay in the game long enough to win.

One young man who played for Hamilton boys high in the final that day, was big and powerful NO 8 Tallis Karaitiana , this is what he had to say ,*Tallis Cheers thanks for all the advice Craig you have really been a help for people in our team and me. Thanks for supporting our team and having faith in us to take out national honours, really means a lot to us winning. Thanks Tallis*

*And representing our school and families, we have always arrived for success by being the hardest working players and most humble, thanks once again*

I ask tallis, what was the difference? Your honest opinion? And did those motivational tips, inspire and influence you? And have some type of bearing on you, and in some way, on your way through to the final? Think about it, they are just a couple of simple questions I wanted to ask you, that's all

*Tallis Yeah, your words were really meaningful and true. Everything that you said to me, you told me to believe in the dream, all influenced me personally as I looked at the game from another perspective, you said 'the difference between an ordinary team and a great team is that the great team will go out give it all, endure till to the end, and overcome the opposition at all costs'. This to me was inspiring and I think it reflected in our performance on Saturday, we definitely wanted it more and got the result because of it.*

**A winner's mentality fuelled by action:** "Talent wins games, but teamwork and intelligence wins championships." --**Michael Jordan.**

# Dream to stay in the game long enough to win.

Here are 12 of successful keynote principles that will help you stay in the game long enough to win.

**1** Preparation.
**2** Perseverance.
**3** Persistence.
**4** Process training skills & strategies
**5** Performances Building winning positions over the season
**6** Endurance staying in the game long enough to win and qualifies you for the reward
7 Response according to the situation
**8** Dare to Dream there is always a price to pay.
To dream, you have to have heart.
**9** Dream /goal/targets.
How big are the teams, dreams/goals so far, are they on the way to hitting their target.
**10** Belief/desire/visualization.
How big is their belief - desire –visualization?
Can they visualize the actually winning now in their minds?
How hungry are the boys to win?
Have the boys got that burning desire?
Are the boys prepared to give that 20% extra for glory?
**11** Mental/Action.
Are the boys ready and willing to take action, do battle and conquer fear, take no prisoners passion –courage –intensity-fear of failures- mistakes- commitment to .Take their passion and motivation, to another level, turn it into to momentum, and get the results they deserve.

**12** Great Leadership - team work-skills- value- , how valuable is every team member from 1 to 22 that take the field, to do battle, thank each and every one in your team, tell them how valuable they are, these are the key building block qualities of great champions.

# Try .P.P.P, so powerful it works every time.

**Questions you may ask your self**

1 How is my persistence and perseverance going so far?
2 How is my passion towards my own dream?
3 How is my discipline?
4 Am I prepared to stay focused and fight for my dream long enough I will win.

How are you going @ work?
How about the Company, Business, Organisation?
How is your family?
How is the team going?
How is the dream?

You may be walking out of a game, sitting on the slide line, or you could be waiting for things to happen, or wonder what happened

If things are working out, then that's great, on the other hand if things aint working out to your satisfaction, then you could always fall back on P.P.P

**Preparation .Perseverance .Persistence** can take you a long way in life, they can help you stay in the game long enough to be a winner.

I love speaking engagements, for many people they would be fearful.

For me the more, I make things happen, I prepare and speak and with perseverance and persistence in front of people, the better and stronger I get. I stay in the game long enough to win

Do you remember the first time you rode your bike, I fell off, more then I got on?

## . Try .P.P.P, so powerful it works every time

<u>A winners mentality fuelled by action:</u> "Energy and persistence conquer all things." -Benjamin Franklin

How many times did you fall off your bike, it's the getting back on, that took, preparation perseverance .persistence, doing it again and again and again , it help me endure long enough to stay in the game and win, the harder I worked to stay on and ride the bike the luckier I got.

Preparation is so vital to all our success in life, if you don't prepare for the challenges ahead, you will find the path will get a little rough and staying in the game long enough will be difficult and you quit end up with little reward and lots of regret.

A Dream is the same, it will never come true, if you don't prepare, persist, have perseverance to carry on, So many people play with their dream, and don't actually work on their dream; their dreams will always be, just be a wish.

**Great Coaches** will tell you, you can't have a winning season, if you're not prepared, to persevere and persist to lay down the ground work and repeat those little skill sets that really count, again, again, again ,for those who do endure, the rewards are fantastic ,it's worth it staying in the game long enough to win.

Use the P.P.P formula today, tomorrow, in future, it so important to your success in life.

Are you still on target to achieve the dream you have always wanted at this time, are you restless, tired, lack motivation, no energy, feel like you want to quit, give up when people say it can't be done, remember to make your dream a reality, ask yourself am I going to keep my dream alive? Keep going, because if I stay focused on my dream, and I know I stay in long enough and endure, I will win.

No matter how many times you fall down in your life it matters how you rise up and get back up again you are the winner

- ## Why successful dreamers do, what they do, never quit.

What is it that dreamers do to become very successful, and potentially reach their goals?

**"They never quit and keep going on and on, until they reach the outcome and destination of what is they are trying to achieve. Successful dreamers believe that failure is not an option"**

Successful dreamers don't just dream about what it is they want, they prepare to win and fight for the dream.

I have a friend who talked about a boxing match, he went to, he was the coach and trainer, this young man he was training ended fighting for the light middle weight junior division national title, this kid had met this top fighter on a few occasions, and he had lost to him several times.

The thing about this kid was, he wanted to challenge himself again and again, not to give in, so as the fight progressed on, this kid was beat up, and took a heavy pounding to the body. This time, he said I give up, I want to give up, im hurting, he's hurting me, I want you to throw the towel in the ring, my friend said don't give up,

**"You have dreamed about this moment for a very long time, this is your time and you have come this far, how do you want to end it, a loser or champion"**

Now listen we need to change tactic, stop your moaning , If you really want to win, you need to take it in to what I am about to say and take control, when he comes into the ring and throws everything at you just hold up, let him come down on to you with his head ,you keep up the defensive, when he lifts up his head, you land him with your power left hook, listen just do it and you will win, guess what he put that left hook to good use and knock the opponent out. The point of this story is

<u>**A winner's mentality fuelled by action:**</u> "Never doubt or count you're self out, go all out to win."

# Why successful dreamers do, what they do, never quit.

Some times in this case it took a lot of hard work, changes of tactic, sweat, pain to gain and win.

I remember a time, my wife and I climbed to the top of Mount Maunganui instead of walking around the base of the mount on the flat, we thought we would take the stairs going straight up the mountain, for others they would have said, that's to much like hard work , im going to go the easy way, we committed and persisted with the journey, there was sweat, drink breaks, stoppages ,our heart rate had climbed, we felt changes in body pain in all places, along with sore legs, going to the top. One of the great signs that came out of this, was our fitness level ,it wasn't that great, our minds had given our bodies a shakeup, **"start to take control of your body and get fit, your journey would have been a much better experience if you planned to start walking or running and exercising first"**, but at the end of all that hard work, was the rewards of the views from the top of the mountain, and we reached the summit, over the next couple of days our bodies were recuperating from the pain of the walk.

What successful dreamers do is they overcome the obstacles and strategize how to get there.

Successful dreamers don't use Excuses as an option, while writing this book is hasn't been easy, because of excuses and distractions.

We have two minds **a sub conscious** and **conscious mind** , one tells us to work hard at what we do, to focus on the task at hand, to get it done before we move on to the next, and to finish it well.

We also have another part of the mind, saying take a break its ok get comfortable, hey what's on TV, im going to stay on the internet for the whole day, and go from face book to YouTube.

We can become our own time wasters, believe me, it is so easy to do, and we become a victim of our own making, instead of making time for our big dream.

# Why successful dreamers do, what they do, never quit.

"We are great at wasting our time doing others things, that don't have any relevance towards the important task we are meant to finish, which leads to a promotion that we deserve, but don't get".

No matter who we are, it's going to happen, it is the nature of humans who think they have the right to treat us unfairly, tell us what to do, with our dreams and lives, we know, we are not all not perfect, get over it, you can either feel sorry for yourself, or push forward and put it behind you – even use it as motivation.

I could use this book as an excuse; I don't feel like writing today, won't be able to be a motivational speaker, im too scared to talk to people. Instead, I see it as an opportunity to learn, grow, and eventually help others all around the world.

We must listen to our own excuses. Understand why we have them, and then figure out how you can use them for the good.

Those 'tangibles Things in life can be a motivator, but it only lasts for so long ,bit like a novelty , they can even be a reward, but things cannot motivate others . The successful dreamer in life always gets there, because they created change in the lives of others, not just their own, they go that extra mile for others

I have friends who have been successful in their lives, and said our success has been to work hard and give it all you're got, you see

They used their time effectively and efficiently and sacrificed, social, family engagements and focus on the mission

Their mission is first and foremost. Until it's complete, everything else comes second.

There's literally no substitute for hard work, because if you get the job done, you will bath in the fruits of your labour.

# Why successful dreamers do, what they do, never quit.

How are your fitness levels, this is really important and I will talk about dreams and fitness, why you should stay healthy, a friend of mine who is a fitness trainer said to me, his clients

**"Want to stay in shape, not only for themselves, also for their work load and better decision making, the fitter we are, the easier it is to focus and think, and the higher in productivity and the quality of our work is".**

Fitness training is a routine part of our lives, it will increases our chances at success – in every meaning of the word

One of Apple's philosophies is to bring change to the world through technology, and they do it with every product they release.

My philosophy is to help inspire to influence others to help themselves to be better and to know how to win, that will help them in life, through tough times, and when things are fantastic.

There have been times in my life when I think of wavering and hopelessly give up. Yet there are those who defy the odds.

We all have moments of doubt. The best of us do question "is our own dream is going to work" "or come true"?

I have moments when I doubt myself and ask, why.

**"The one thing that separates the truly successful dreamer from those who never reach their true potential is an unbreakable chain belief in fact, that what they're doing is right, they know they have a plan of direction and cease the outcome" C.D Walden**

# Why successful dreamers do, what they do, never quit.

Even now when I first started writing winner circle of dreams, if I have moments of doubt now, they're soon squashed, people didn't believe in me, I was crazy, mad, only the few believed, I know of others friends who had dreams, listen to that doubt and let others manipulate their mind-set, it ate them up and finally they quit.

Yes we have our moments of doubt. We are human. I don't let doubt eat me up. Instead I let it motivate me to lead me to a bigger and brighter outcome

**The reason to endure.**

Many of the successful dreamer's greatest accomplishments in the world were accomplished by reason, they had a reason inside, entrenched in their hearts, that was so powerful, the reason made them live, eat, breathe and endure, they had something to prove to others. The reason created change that was so strong, that failure in their eyes was simply never an option.

The great American migration from the East Coast of America to open up the wild wild west of California the sunny state, many had a reason and a dream, endured, survived while others literally died, or quit. A lot of people didn't make it, not because they were bad, the ones that made it, were fortunate, but they were the best because of what they endured. You see when you endure, it meant never give up never quit, to the end, and simply be the last ones standing.

**A winner's mentality fuelled by action:** "Sometimes we don't know when our breakthrough in life will come. So don't guarantee your failure by quitting or buy your current condition. You can adapt, change, and evolve, but never, never, never quit".

# Why successful dreamers do, what they do, never quit.

Did you know you can learn from the best, Successful dreamers learn from Great Masters?

Bruce lee studied his craft as much as anyone in the martial arts. Bruce lee spent hours upon hours studying opposing grand masters in the art of kung fu. He studied their patterns. He's known for his speed and agility and physical presence, became the top martial arts movie idol of all time, Bruce lee crafted his work to be the best at what he was good at, he was always a student first and grand performance movie star second, Bruce never gave up and also excelled to be the best in his field

Today lot of top sports athletes and teams have grafted their skill from learning from the best in their field, by reading books, watching the best game plays. How we get better is by learning from other great grand masters of sport, business, study, is what made them so great, if you want to be the next big basketball player on the block, take a look at Michael Jordan, Larry bird they practised their craft every day, 500 free throws, they knew, they always had the winning edge against their opposition They learnt to be students first and the masters of basketball second.

Writing the winner's circle of dreams is exciting, and to get better, I simply read great books written by proven authors, who know how to write, listen to great audios of great speakers, I learn my craft from them. Remember no one has ever achieved any greatness on their own.

"I truly believe successful big dreamers that have become successful worldwide, have studied and perfected their craft from other grand masters of success learn it inside and out. Successful dreamers build a wealth of knowledge that helps them create a great, inspiring, and unique winning edge".

I have taken a risk, have you, one key ingredient successful dreamers have is those who have achieved real success have often risked the most to get there.

# Why successful dreamers do, what they do, never quit.

I know for me right now, I am taking the big risk ,that once I write this book ,and do motivational speaking that everything will fall into place , I haven't finished the book yet and haven't started to speak, I have risk so much ,less money, being,

stuck in a 1 bedroom flat with my teenage daughter sleeping on the floor, some days its feels like I have lost everything, wind back the clock, remember I talked about Jim Cary a few chapters back, I love his story, before he became the superstar he was, he hung around Hollywood <u>with no money</u> and <u>was stone broke, nowhere to sleep</u> and <u>a fake check note</u>, he kept in his wallet, pretending he was already a millionaire

   **"Jim Cary <u>got turned down and rejected so many times</u>, he was feeling the same way I do, In the end the dream and risk, perseverance, persistence prevailed and won ,that paid off. Someone hired this crazy outrageous funny man and gives him a check worth 10,000.000, he didn't give up, it's like you have to take that risk to do something, if you don't take that risk, you will never know the outcome".**

Successful dreamers throughout history who have had the ability to achieve greatness, whether it was the gifts and talent but one thing is for sure they never quit,

Many people say they don't have the guts to risk the life that they really want to live, will never see their potential and life fulfilled, because they are too comfortable One of saddest tragedy in life is wasted talent, I now realize, I am so glad I did Xfactor I didn't win it, but I know I was the winner in the end, because I was prepared to dream and take the risk learn and craft my talent

Find your dream. Then risk everything to get it.

<u>**A winner's mentality fuelled by action:**</u> "I never gave up believing, because I knew who I could become "me" **Funny man Jim Cary.**
No matter how many times you fall down in your life it matters how you rise up and get back up again you are the winner.

- # Guard your Dream, Mind, Body, and Heart at all times.

My immune system protects me how about you
Recently I went to the doctors, I think I was coming down with the so called flu, and so my doctor said I had a sore throat .I had the symptoms and he said, I can't give you anything for it because it's only a virus now, if you were coughing, I would gave you antibiotics.

I said to the doctor, what do I do doc, he said, just rest up, your immune system will take care of the virus, the immune response is how your body recognizes and defends itself against bacteria, viruses, and substances that appear foreign and harmful

Isn't this the same, we must guard not only our body, our big dreams, goals, our mind and our heart, you could get spellbound or people will overload your mind full of negativity, it will break your heart and mind, so it's hard to be that person, you want to be, and know who you really are

I know so, it is so true, we have to be so careful and aware of what we let take hold of us, though our hearts and minds, our immune system ,is much in the same way, it is vigilant 24 hours a day to protect the body from the, viruses ,disease substances.

I have an obligation to finish this book and not get side-tracked because sometimes it can happen, you say you want to achieve things, start of doing it ,and then turn around you don't finish, what you set to do ,what you knew you were capable of,

but you didn't get there, because somebody hurt you, stole your dream, told you a lie, something derailed you, and you let your mind and heart say yes to what ever happened, we live in a society of compounding and changing technology and newspaper media cyberspace fuelled with so many things that have a major bearing and influence on the way our mind thinks and what we put into our hearts.

# My immune system protects me how about you

**Do you really want to follow others and let them influence you, or do you want to find out who you really are C.D WALDEN**

Deception of who you think you are is preventing you from experiencing the greater discovery of who you really are.

**A winners mentality fuelled by action:** "If there are obstacles in your life right now, Chances are, you are "Affected by doubt, bad attitude and destructive distractions of what people have said"

Guard your mind and heart to overcome mental strongholds, breakout of negative thought and finally sidestep the poisonous traps that snare you into a life of struggle and defeat.

# Wear protective clothing 24/7

**Wear protective clothing 24/7**

I have a friend who has served in the army for 20 years; they practice warfare situations, and prepare themselves to do battle against the resisters

**I know his teams go on full alert, and are equipped with helmets and bullet proof vests, stay vigilant at all times, prepared for any type of sniper resistance and encounter from the enemy**

It's the same with in our everyday lives, heard of that song life is a battle field

**Mental toughness "We need to put on our coat of armour helmet and bulletproof" body, mind, heart, so negative snipers bullets won't be able infiltrate to cause destruction, despair, doubt and derail or even sivitarge your mission in life"**

The mind must be protected, be vigilant, because like people if they get the chance to infiltrate your mind , the mind breaks inside you and leads to lies you are been told about yourself, your past, your future, your possibilities .

You ever felt horrible inside, someone said nasty things about you, you know literately your emotions in your heart and mind at that time, the good image you had about yourself is literately disappeared

Like the army We must keep our armour on us at all times because 24 hours day we live a life battle world and at times try not to get to comfortable and take our equipment off , we need to endure and survive for our own benefit because there are snipers all around ready and waiting to pick you off.

# Wear protective clothing 24/7

I know bullets can kill instantly and injuries have the power to leave battle scars forever in one's heart.

I also believe if you get injured you can get fixed again and your condition can change too for the better.

Our minds are like that as well, we have been picked off by sniper bullets at some stage of our lives, and didn't bother to leave our amour of steel on, so we have paid the price, because we were so casual about things and now we have to deal with our injuries and bandage them up so our condition can be better.

My friend said to me when you live in the war zone you have to learn to adapt pretty quickly, you have to keep the enemy abbey, they will try to get in ,to stay in, Who wants to be a captive and a prisoner of war and controlled mentally and physically, you get caught by the enemy, then what happen is there is total interrogation infiltration it doesn't matter on what grounds you negotiate to the enemy they will control you mentally and physically, create strangle holds and take over your house, home , and army base .

**<u>A winner's mentality fuelled by action:</u>** "In the middle of difficulties lies, an opportunity" – **Albert Einstein**

## Diamonds in rough still they shine

The other day I was reading an article about people and their fascination with Diamonds ever heard of the saying diamonds are girl's best friend, yes they are a real gem for woman of the world who love them, i done some research and found out that, A diamond is a life solid hunk of rock a diamond isn't light, it only reflects light, so we see a diamond, we see the light reflecting of that, it lets you know it's a diamond Someone go to a jewellery shop and ask a jeweller , he can tell you the difference between a fake diamond, and a real diamond based on how it goes reflecting the light. "Diamonds are formed deep within the rough of the Earth, and it takes a lot of time (usually few billion years) for diamonds to be formed when unearthed, most diamonds appear roughly rounded with perhaps a hint of regular crystal form. Many are colourless, but most are pale shades of yellow; red, orange, green, blue, brown, and even black diamonds are also found. Raw, uncut stones lack the exuberance of jewellery-store gems and can appear quite ordinary;

A diamond isn't like life itself; it will only reflect the light.

A famous comet called Halley's Comet which lights up the earth's sky every 76years isn't like life itself, but a massive hunk of ice, it will only reflect the light from the sun.

Human beings are so unique too, there is only one of you; you have the power to reflect your shining light to others.

**"Your mind and heart will change if you are living along side or in darkness, doom and gloom, doubt, negativity, so how can your uniqueness possibly reflect the light of truth about you".**

You see your mind works in the same way as a diamond ,if your mind thinks, hears and sees all of the darkness around you, then you will project darkness inside of you.

# Diamonds in rough still they shine

I tell my kids they are a diamonds, and to let them know, they are unique, there is only one diamond like them that produces a magnificent shining light, whether you are going through tough times, even in the rough times of life, you need to magnify your shining light

Most amazingly A diamond can be buried in darkness, beneath the earth's crust and surface and it still come out of its location ,and still hasn't changed it life form amazingly it still reflects a shining light .


**A winner's mentality fuelled by action:** "Keep away from the small minded people who try to belittle your ambitions, small minded people always do that, but the really great make you feel that you too can become great"- **Mark Twain**

# Guard your Dream, Mind, Body, and Heart at all times.

Guard your mind and heart ,keep your body in top shape don't abuse it ,be the vigilant protector , crack shot enemy snipers are all round in business , relationship , friends ,family, community, to take you out, to pierce your heart and mind ,take away your uniqueness of who you really are, and capture you, and lead you into darkness , be proactive and aware ,you have a choice to recognize it, if you rather or realize it or not. Don't believe the myth, everyone is your friend in life, or will like you; they can make life difficult, causing your mind into recession and depression and your heart go to into emotional heartache and despair for you, if you let them.

Questions you may ask yourself
**1** Do I have to live with negativity?
**2** How do I cope with things said about my past, present?
**3** Does my personality show the true reflection of, who I really know I can be?

**4** I want to get out of the doom and gloom mind trap, is there a way out?

**<u>A winner's mentality fuelled by action:</u>** "picture yourself vividly as winning and that alone will contribute immeasurably on the road to your success"- **Henry Fosdick**

# Guard your Dream, Mind, Body, and Heart at all times.

Here are 10 Keynote winners circle of dreams tips to guard your, body, mind, heart
**1** Eliminates negative thoughts, you win
**2** Cut ties with negative relationships and influences, you win
**a** Drugs, you win
**b** Gambling, you win
**c** Bad Food, you win
**d** TV, you win
**E** Internet gaming, addictions some of us have relationships with these things .we all have had a relationship with it somewhere in life

**3** Get rid of negative emails
**4** Bad cyber media
**5** Horrible Cards and letters
**6** Bad Friends
**7** Gossip
**8** People who don't respect you
**9** Disengage from bad relationships that support negativity
**10** Get rid of bad voice mail & text bullies

No matter how many times you fall down in your life it matters how you rise up and get back up again you are the winner.

# • Share your big dreams with the butterfly not with the spider.

One of my favourite seasons is spring time, you know when the cold winter days and nights are on the way out, we get excited and start with our spring cleaning, we are heading into longer days and warmer temperatures, filled with big smiles.

Aint it funny that humans sense a change coming, there is that big buzz, of anticipation, even the insects and gardens ,flowers ,birds start to come alive . You know spring is in the air, have you ever watched the monarch butterfly, so busy flying around seemingly ever so graceful, they have such an awesome attitude, they're such beautiful creatures with colourful orange and black wings, Can you ever image it's amazing, that this butterfly emerges from ugly little caterpillar, to a cocoon, then emerges as a butterfly that is so unique.

The monarch would be so proud of itself, if it could see its beauty in the mirror.

The adult butterfly consumes all sorts of different things including sweet nectar, water and even liquids from some of the fruits, banana, oranges, and watermelon.

A monarch season of life is so limited and short, that they make the most of all the opportunities they have been given

Monarch butterflies fly around freely, they go about minding their business, hurting no one, they are such innocent creatures with such a great attitude. We live and admire and adore them. We as humans can learn from the butterfly of its beauty, gracefulness and of it innocents and how they show us how busy and active they really are.

**<u>A winners mentality fuelled by action</u>:** "it's in your moment of decision that your destiny takes shape" – **Anthony Robbins**

# Share your big dreams with the butterfly not with the spider.

## The monarch fills us with dreams, hope and new fresh light of a new spring day.

The spring season in the animal and insect kingdoms are about survival, although butterflies have the love, charm, beauty, gracefulness, innocents minding their own business, it is some of these instincts that make them become vulnerable to become the hunted and target from predators, which have come out of the winter hibernation who are very hungry and need energy and sustenance .

Top of the list predators for the butterfly is the spider, have you seen the ways a spider operates, in the spiders domain it spins a silk web to captor its victims, once caught in the web, the spider it will win, and takes full advantage and control, the victims chance of breaking free from the web, which is pretty remote, that you will come out alive, you see spiders don't kill you straight away they paralyse you with poison first, even if the victims who are 10 times bigger than them, will be at the mercy of the spider .just think of this, a spiders has kidnapped you and they wrap you up in silk thread and store you away and think about, what they are going to do with you later.

Spiders keep busy poisoning other insects the community as well, what a wonderful career they have killing all their victims slowly, and make a meal and turn on their partners as well

<u>The Spider & the Butterfly Attitude Theory</u>
The monarch butterfly act in a different manner to the spider, both have a different attitude and approach towards to which they do business with others in the insect kingdom.

Don't mess around with spiders you could end up on the wrong side of the ledger spider filled with, poison, paralyze and full bitterness.

# Share your big dreams with the butterfly not with the spider.

With humans it can be the same, we can have a monarch butterfly attitude or people will take on the spider's attitude and make a misery of people's lives and inject them with the poison of bitterness.

Do you know of people with the spider attitude that are willing to take you out with their poison?

Spiders attitude have the ability to strike everywhere; they could be in the community church, clubs friends, work mates, family at any time.

Do you have friends and family , work colleges who point the finger at you, say the gossip things about you, quick at pointing out your weakness and yet they really don't know what you are capable of ,these are people with the spider attitude ,believe me there are plenty of them out there

Have you ever shared your big dreams or started out getting excited about something you told the spiders, because if you have, chances are, you experienced getting caught up in the spiders web 1 paralyzed, 2 poisoned and full of bitterness, 3 the big dream you had in your heart died of a slow death and turned into liquid.

"Take up the monarch butterfly winners attitude ,time is so precious , they are so active with self-confidence I would rather fly around with a great attitude and staying busy and making a difference, helping to inspire and influence in others' lives and bringing out the best in people",

Than staying around people who take up the spider's attitude who are bullies, very nasty and have no respect for others.

**A winners mentality fuelled by action:** "Your attitude is everything' - **Jim Rohn**

No matter how many times you fall down in your life it matters how you rise up and get back up again you are the winner

# CHAPTER 6 NOTES

# Chapter 7

## • No Excuses, No Excuses, No Excuses Start Wining Today.

Aint family great, even though I am a husband and farther ,I still am accountable for my actions, well my wife and daughter had questioned me, " how long is it going to take to finish the book" winners circle of dreams, that I couldn't answer straight away, I knew I was on the right track and putting little bits and pieces of my book together, I then started to question myself about the time, and what I have been doing with it, and here's what I come with, and it's so true, <u>Am I too comfortable</u>, 2 <u>Am pushing myself hard enough.</u>

3 Have I put a time line in place to finish winner's circle of dreams, or do I need take responsibility because I have been lazy and irresponsible and done little to show my progress for moving forward. I am saying this to you

**"in the life of real business , you want to keep your job these days there's no place for excuses, time is money and time is wasted, if you were on face book in work time and you're not really focused on the companies work ,it can become an excuse"**

Means that Facebook take more president over your job, that is why most companies have kpi = **key performance indicators** and **micro managing** in place for their employees to **measure performance** in the work place.

Getting back to my wife and family, I am so glad they take the time talk with me to ask me how I am going, they are concerned in a good way, they just want to see me achieve and finish the winner circle of dreams, bosses are the same, they voice their concern if they know their employee is not performing well. **We all as humans do this, we all use the excuse word, there have been days where I could have done a lot better and I knew it, my excuse took over, but I know I didn't use the time wisely and**

# No Excuses, No Excuses, No Excuses Start Wining Today.

effectively enough while on the internet flicking through the websites and other media

It going to take too much time, sometimes we look at time as the root of all evil,

With time, we tend to do the time thing, we want to do, and not the important time things, that needed to be done. With a lot of time on your hands can also be trouble for excuses.

So many people have too much time on their hands, and are actually doing nothing productive for their future, I can be honest, im only human, and we all have done it at some time in our lives.

Our Excuses can stop us from progressing and going forward in our lives, big dreams and goals can be fuelled in the same way also, we will never to be able to know how much potential we have inside of us. We have to let go of those habits of excuses.

Here are some of the top 10 potential excuses everybody uses, we should quit making excuses

**1** That dream and goal are too big for me.
**2** Too tied up right now
**3** Im too busy doing nothing, but still too busy
**4** I can't do that
**5** No maybe I will do it tomorrow
**6** Fears and failure, I will leave it to ponder over another time
**7** My hands are full with the kids tonight
**8** My diaries full
**9** Something's come up
**10** Its summer holidays now
I will wait for that new product to come out
I found out, we can use other people's excuses and blame them for our demise, in fact honestly I can say

**"The key is to check ourselves and take responsibility and we are obligated to do just that, so many people use excuses/problem because it's a way of getting out of something that really needs to be addressed themselves"**

# No Excuses, No Excuses, No Excuses Start Wining Today.

but is put into one side of their to do hard basket of their lives. Have you ever run out of gas before, I can tell you it's no fun when you are stuck in the middle of nowhere with a bunch of kids in the car that's run out of gas on the side of the road, its happened to my wife and I, you can't use an excuse, and say I will leave it there tomorrow, you have to address the problem, and go and get some gas from the petrol station, how you get there to the gas station, you have to make a responsible decision, you will find a way.

We all are ready to do something special for our own lives, but are we willing to make the changes from excuses, to be able to gain possibilities

Whatever we do try to do in our life, Excuses will reveal our weaknesses, and demonstrate our unwillingness, to put what it is we would like to do, into action.

**"We as human beings seem to think we are incapable of greatness, or that our dreams are impossible to reach, and is merely a cover-up excuse, for avoiding personal responsibility, confronting our fears and critics, and retracting from the work success requires".**

Elimination of excuses can be fixed, try some of the key principles tips and tell me how you get on

Here are 11 Keynote winners circle of dreams tips to eliminate excuses
**1** Eliminate worry and fear they produce excuses
**2** Be true to yourself, find out what it is that's on your mind
**3** Find out what excuses is holding you back
**4** If you stay busy, focus and try taking action on your big dream today, you will find there is no time for excuses to appear in your life, excuses will disappear

5 **You don't have to take on board somebody else's excuse, it belong to them and not you.**

# No Excuses, No Excuses, No Excuses Start Wining Today.

**6** Be adventurous do something that's different

**7** Be aware of your excuses, but don't dwell in excuses or even contemplating hosting your excuses

**8** You must make time for your big dreams excuses will lead you to nowhere

**9** Don't let the excuse control you, you take control of it, take responsibility

**10** The quickest way to beat an Excuse is to dissolve it

**11** Write you excuse down on paper, is this so important it's only a thought; you can eliminate your excuses any time by seeing and dealing with them and crossing them of your list.

<u>**A winner's mentality fuelled by action**</u>: "The critical ingredient to beating excuses is to get off your butt and do something about it; it's as simple as that. A lot of people have great ideas, but there a few who decide to do something about them today , not tomorrow , not next week , but now"- **Nolan Bushnell**

No matter how many times you fall down in your life it matters how you rise up and get back up again you are the winner.

## • Dreams can become Obstacles v obligation = Dreams can become opportunity.

Some body ask me about excuses and said "are excuses the same as obstacles"? Here is what I had to say

**"Excuses are nothing more than a thought of lies that fear and failure has sold you, Obstacles are something's that stands in the way and makes passage or progress difficult"**

.We as humans combat obstacles, have an obligation in order to create opportunity to conquer. Pursuing what you want to do in life to get what you want .Everyone in life, will have face ups and a face down crisis while you are on your journey and you come across the obstacles path, and are expecting the worst, visualize the obstacle, and find that solution, find your why, the opportunity will arise, keep going, on the path of opportunity and celebrate each small step, you will arrive at the finish line of success with a renewed confidence in your ability, to set out and fulfil your big dream and aspirations.

**"Successful dreamers Focus on opportunity, you may have an obstacle standing in your way, but don't base your decision**

**on fear remember seek strategies, you can always weave your way inside and outside and around the obstacle course of life, obstacles with a strategies create an opportunity"**

As people in the community we spend a great deal of our time dealing with and trying to solve obstacles

**Successful businesses , sports people ,leaders major companies are responsible and take matters in their own hands ,they find a solution to their obstacle, and don't dwell on what's not and can't be done rather than, see the obstacle as an opportunity to create good from it .**

## • Dreams can become Obstacles v obligation = Dreams can become opportunity.

My thoughts are I believe the outcome from the obstacle is all about was is possible, not what's impossible, there are times in our lives when we reactive obstacles and magnify them into something like a barbed wire fence that's been enclosed, that is too hard to fix or face, and we are left dwelling in the negative and we end up finding no solution to the obstacles, we need to reactive our own obstacles and turn them into opportunities, and not deactivate our obstacles and leave them in heart of our life and do nothing about them

Those People with Big dreams are so powerful and know what they want , where they are going , the big dreamers are not fazed by obstacles, to them are nothing new they can be moved with a mountain of faith hope and strategies and creativity, and the will to push forward and clear path on the way to success

**"My dad always said to me there are many obstacles and they may seem big at the time but learn what's best to cease the bigger opportunities from them".**

Ever been and played on an obstacle course, it works on the same principles, there are many obstacles in the way and you have to find a way to 1 go around them 2 inside and out 3 over the top,

first, you work out or strategize the best way to create an opportunity to get on the other side of the obstacle.

When you finish the Obstacles course, did you remember how you felt, you had the opportunity to showcase your talents and abilities. As Human beings we are special and unique in our own way how are we ever going to able to demonstrate our capabilities and have a major bearing where we are at in our own lives, without obstacles it's kind of like being an exceptional rugby sports team. No one really knows how good you are until you operate against the pressure of resisters who are the opposite team.

## • Dreams can become Obstacles v obligation = Dreams can become opportunity.

"Obstacles are in our lives for a reason they help us rise above to challenge our own level of expectation"

If we fear obstacles, we will live of fear, but we if face up, raise up and jump over, weave inside and out and find a way around obstacles we will conquer them, you will start to get comfortable and confident and strong, your fear will be no more and then you will find out who you truly are.

Have you ever watched the ant and how they overcome obstacles, I was sitting down in my chair on the driveway next to the garage, it was a long and hot summers day, I was eating my lunch and I noticed a whole bunch of ants marching up and down near my feet, I had spilt sticky bread crumbs everywhere, before I knew it, the ants were crawling on the concrete drive way, carrying the bread crumbs heading in one direction they ended up all over my feet, under my feet and around my feet

Ants are amazing creatures they are great workers and team players ,even the size of my feet which became the obstacle for them didn't deter them from getting their chores done ,they were determined   just kept going over, under and around my feet

**Doesn't matter how big the obstacles are for ants, I can assure you for their size and never say die character, guts, courage and determination ,ants cease opportunity ,they will just keep going and never give up, the ant will always find a way to get around an obstacle. They haven't got time for an obstacle to detract them from their busy working life**

## Dreams can become Obstacles v obligation = Dreams can become opportunity.

## "Don't let your obstacles be a hindrance an obstruction to your winning circle of dreams and success" CD Walden

Conquer the obstacle course of life today, be like the ants don't quit, cease the opportunity weave your way inside, outside, over and around your obstacles •

Questions you may want to ask yourself.
1 I need to identify my obstacles
2 How can I do this?
3 Can I ask for help?
4 If I overcome my obstacles, what's in it for me

Here are 10 keynote winners circle of dream tips to help overcome obstacles
1 You have obstacles face them head on
2 Treat your obstacle as a challenge
3 Find strategies solutions to help overcome your obstacle
4 Obstacles seek and create opportunity
5 Don't make your obstacle any bigger than it really is
6 You can always ask someone about the same obstacle, they went through and how they overcame it

7 There is always a way around, inside, outside, and over, obstacles, ask the ant

8 Obstacles measure ones true dedication and persistence

9 Your Obstacle didn't say to you don't quit, your obstacle just said move me out of the way

10 Grab a pen and paper write down your obstacles that way you can see them, you take responsibility and control over them,

## Dreams can become Obstacles v obligation = Dreams can become opportunity.

"An obstacle course is the same, you see the course, but you make the moves to get to the other side"

<u>**A winner's mentality fuelled by action :**</u> "Obstacles are those frightful things you can see, if don't have a goal, if you take your eyes of the goal in life"- **Henry Ford**

No matter how many times you fall down in your life it matters how you rise up and get back up again you are the winner.

# • I did whatever it takes to get to the grand final

Remember the ant story how I said the ants love to challenge obstacles and weave inside, outside over the top and around them because the key is action, determination, courage, belief, persistence and perseverance and endurance they will strategize a way to win to get to their destination, same goes with life its self, a big dream or goal how far are you prepared to go, to get what it is you really want.

Recently in 2012 I managed the go to Super 15xv rugby grand final which was held in Hamilton NZ .What a great final it was between the Chiefs Super Rugby Franchise from New Zealand and the Natal Sharks Super Rugby Franchise from South Africa, I was so glad I could be there to watch history been written, for a lot of people to witness the success of the chiefs winning actually being at the live game is so awesome, only few had that pleasure to experience for a life time.

I am going to rewind back the clock, and tell you about the considerable effort and time it took to go because in reality it should not have happened at all. **"The outcome was great ending, anyone can relate to that, but what people don't realize is the process of how, whether there was a game to go to from the beginning, as this was one true blue obstacle"**

The tickets for the game were sold out online, as well as the usual booking outlets, so where do I start, I needed the ant instincts to help me overcome the obstacle of how to a get a game ticket first .

At the beginning of finals week, Radio and TV and other media Networks had said, there were no tickets left for the final, they mentioned people ticket scouting, selling them on trade me or on the black market for an exorbitant price would be void and in trouble with the law, after hearing that advice, I had given myself the doubt there is no way I could possibly be going, how could I even contemplate being there, I had no money to buy the ticket anyway, so that dream I thought was short lived done and dusted.

# I did whatever it takes to get to the grand final

3 days before the finals my daughter had heard that a radio station had 4 double pass promotional game tickets throughout the country to give away, she rang me and told me, "but dad you have to listen on the radio station when they ask u to ring them at the station you have to be in to win".

Wow I thought this would be a great chance to win a ticket if I could get through, but I also knew that every man and his dog throughout New Zealand were doing the same thing, glued to the radio and wanting those tickets just as much as me, my chances were pretty slim. Did you think I could sleep that night? Answer "no," I didn't, not for the next two day at least, I know during those nights, **"I dreamed and visualized I could see myself at the game, the excitement & atmosphere was electric.**

**I started to believe, I was in with a chance to win those tickets just as much as anyone else, I could already feel the tickets in the palm of my hand, I believed it was my destiny and I wasn't about to give up no matter what it takes".**

That Thursday morning week of the final, the radio station were giving away 4 double pass tickets, between 7am and 9am they started to give the tickets away, when they said your chance to win tickets to the game now, the lines were hot, I tried to get through on the phone, but it was engaged that morning, I counted the number of people who managed to get on the station, 15 people had a chance to win, out of the 15 people who tried , 3 answered the right questions, at the end of that morning there was 1 double pass left, the radio station announcers said to everybody try again tomorrow, we have 1 double pass left, how did I feel, you guessed it "despondent", here we go again, a night without sleep, I still believed I could still be in to win, I revert back to my parents who reminded me about that do or die attitude that help me through, they said it aint over till the fat lady sings, don't right her off because of her size, she has faith and knows who she is and what she is capable of ,the power SOUL voice of Ella Fitzgerald.

# I did whatever it takes to get to the grand final

That night I started to dream again about me being there at Waikato Stadium sitting amongst a full capacity crowd.

Friday morning at 835am I tried my luck to get through on the phone, it didn't happen, but guess what, there had been 8 people that had try to answer the announcers questions, but without success, I was so glad, be that didn't fix the problem, I still didn't have a ticket, my dream of a secured ticket was still a long way off.

Be listening and call back in 10 minutes, we have got the last double pass and hopefully someone has got the right answer to win that ticket.

8.55am I was ready ,it was my last chance , I dialled through to the station, it was engaged, so far 2 people had got through and answered the questions, still no one could give the right answer kept hanging on to the phone and it was still engaged and a third person jumped on the line and she couldn't answer the right question, all of a sudden the phone was dialling through, they said hello, I went all quiet, who is speaking, slowly and taking a deep breathe, "I said Brian" Brian we have got 3 questions for you to answer to win these tickets, to see history being made between the chiefs v sharks, are you ready.

$1^{st}$ question, who is the chiefs' coach? I said Dave Rennie.

$2^{ND}$ Question Brian, "the chiefs came $2^{nd}$ in round robin for 2012 that was ahead of them on the points table"? ,Brian, your answer please 'the Stormers", correct Brian, knowing I was 1 question away, my dream still felt so far away, but in reality in my head I still had that last hurdle to climb, to answer the last question, Brian are you ready, last question, if you get this right, you my friend, will win a double pass to the super rugby final between the chiefs and the sharks, here is the question, my heart was beating fast and really pounding I knew this was the moment of all moments, make or break, the chiefs were in the final back in 2009 in South Africa who did they lose too?

# I did whatever it takes to get to the grand final

Brian your answer please, I replied quietly and I said "the bulls" I waited, then they said, guess what, you have won, then it was all on, my whole household and radio station erupted with elation, laughter and tears of joy I was the winner on the day, I had worked real hard to sit by the phone, taken the action to be persistent and have perseverance to believe and never give up against all odds, I had achieved the unthinkable, I was on my way to the game, I won the tickets, but my journey of how to get the tickets into my hands was another story

Here is a list of 15 keynote action things; I needed to do to go to the game.

**1** I could take a risk; Get on the phone and into the game first, did I get lucky, or was I prepared to endure and work hard

**2** Answer 3 questions, and give the right answers

**3** Endure the frustration that someone would give right answers.

**4** Answer the 3 questions and win.

**5** Radio Station said I had to collect the tickets from the radio station personally

**6** I was in Tauranga so I had to go to Auckland and get the tickets

**7** I rang the radio station and said, can't you put them in the post, and their reply was, no you have to collect personally

**8** If you have won tickets, it's sometimes harder to get them in your hand.

**9** Put Strategies in place; I made 20 phone calls, Radio Station, Couriers, My daughter

**10** My daughter picked the tickets up in Auckland on my behalf before 5pm

**11** That Friday my Daughter courier the tickets down to Tauranga from Auckland.

# I did whatever it takes to get to the grand final

**12** Courier tickets arrived in Tauranga at 245 pm Saturday game day

**13** Got tickets in my hand, how was I going to get to Hamilton and see the game, I had no money.

**14** Go to game with brother in-law, I gave him one of the tickets, in return, he paid for the gas to get us to go and see the final.

**15** I am finally at the game sitting down, and dreaming the dream to watch history in the making.

Yes, we will do, what it takes to achieve, dream big, we all can do anything to have what it is, we would like to have, sometime we can sit back and wait for things to happen, we really would love for our dreams and life to change, the reality is

**"we have to be responsible and action what it is we need to do to make it happen, I would never have been able to be at the game, at first it was just a dream, that's all it could have been if I didn't bother to take action, I did whatever it takes to get to the grand finale, you too can achieve those things possible in your life"**


**A winners mentality fuelled by action:** "I couldn't wait for my tickets to the game of success, so I went ahead without it"- **Jonathan Winters**

No matter how many times you fall down in your life it matters how you rise up and get back up again you are the winner.

- # I will Enjoy Today I will Plan for Tomorrow.

Do you really want to know, how I felt after that live game, I went to see yesterday against the Chiefs verses Sharks Super XV Final 2012, it was tremendous and exciting, today it feels great, when you work hard towards something today, you will see benefit from the rewards tomorrow.

So why can't that happen to you

**"There are always going to be those sceptics who say, tomorrow will never come, reason why, they never planned to do anything about looking ahead to tomorrow at all"**

Yes I will do something today, and they leave things for never, I can tell you in this moment and time if you want to enjoy today and enjoy tomorrow you can

Here are 2 keynote winners of circle tips to feel better today than you did yesterday

**<u>1 Plan for tomorrow.</u>**
**<u>2 Enjoy today.</u>**

In life's reality, the one and only formula to a Plan of success is put your practise into action and teach. This is what success business, corporations, Entrepreneurs, champions do**,** basketball players in the NFL like Michael Jordon and Larry bird, and why they were so good at what they did, and shut teams out of a game, their success formula , practice, practice, practice, repeat, repeat, repeat, they learnt to master the process and performance to produce a winning outcome, time and time again.

# I will Enjoy Today I will Plan for Tomorrow.

Practise, practise, practise, and repeat, repeat, repeat, you must take action today.

1 I will enjoy the fruits of today'
2 I need to plant the seeds for tomorrow, will go running
3 I will enjoy the fruits of today'
4 I need to plant the seeds for tomorrow, will stay healthy, and join the gym
5 I will enjoy the fruits of today'
6 I need to plant the seeds for tomorrow, will get an education, and finish my degree
7 I will enjoy the fruits of today'
8 I need to plant the seeds for tomorrow, will finish of my book, and publish it
9 I will enjoy the fruits of today'
10 I need to plant the seeds for tomorrow, will get job, and get a promotion
11 I will enjoy the fruits of today'
12 I need to plant the seeds for tomorrow, will strengthen my relationship, with my family
13 I will enjoy the fruits of today'
14 I need to plant the seeds for tomorrow, will learn serve, to love, have faith and find happiness
15 I will enjoy the fruits of today'
16 I need to plant the seeds for tomorrow, will plan to financially be debt free
17 I will enjoy the fruits of today'
18 I need to plant the seeds for tomorrow, will write down my dreams and goals
19 I will enjoy the fruits of today'
20 I need to plant the seeds for tomorrow, will say what I say, do what it is I said I would do, when will I do it

I have found out that if I am consistent and action something today, I know that action will set me up to be the winner for tomorrow.

# I will Enjoy Today I will Plan for Tomorrow.

Sports people and Marathon runners prepare and condition themselves for their race and games daily and look forward to tomorrows triumph.

Doctors know the receptionist has made appointments for his /her clients today and the doctor will be looking forward to seeing their client tomorrow.

**Great business and leaders have always enjoyed the fruits of today's success and planted the seed for tomorrow's successful harvest.**

You ever seen your niece or nephew or your own children walking for the first time in their lives, they get up and walk today, and then they are thinking about tomorrow and how far they can walk because, they don't want to crawl around on the flood anymore, they just want today, get walking, and tomorrow explore new frontiers, climb on the couch and make a mess they want to plan their today and tomorrow and have loads of fun doing it

Today im enjoying the victory of yesterday's harvest looking back on what I have achieved writing and finishing the insert, I did whatever it takes to get to the final. It's so unbelievable that I have actually achieved this.

If you are struggling with your big dream or you have obstacles to sort out, maybe it time to look at what you could be doing that's having an effect , today is the today to do whatever it takes to go forward in your life, all you have to do is take control and be willing and find a strategy, you can always fix things to go forward and not look backwards As long as you are doing something now today in your planting the seed for tomorrow, you will come out on top to be the big winner.

# I will Enjoy Today I will Plan for Tomorrow.

Questions you may want to ask.

**1** What have I planned for today?
**2** Am I planning to do something?
**3** I enjoy today, how successful can I be, if I plan and plant the seeds for tomorrow
**4** Im not doing anything at all with my life right now, can someone give me some advice?

Here are 10 POWERFUL keynote winners of circle of dreams benefits from planting a seed tomorrow and enjoy today.

**1** Plant a positive seed for big dreams and goals tomorrow, you will reap a positive harvest of today

**2** Plant a seed today, writing your dreams and goals down on paper, you will be able to allocate time to them, and know what direction you are taking in your life

**3** If you know what you are doing today and tomorrow. You have control of your life
**4** Your attitude will change
**5** A little baby takes its first walk today and will take greater steps tomorrow
**6** I know if I plan for today and tomorrow I will be able to make better decisions
**7** You will feel successful about the future
**8** Get excited and motivated
**9** Planning for tomorrow and today will give you peace of mind
**10** Success and winning are about planting the seed for tomorrow so you can enjoy the fruits of today.

**A winner's mentality fuelled by action:** "when you finally get to the real word meaning of plan & succeed, you find it simply means you must follow through"- **F W Nichol**

No matter how many times you fall down in your life it matters how you rise up and get back up again you are the winner

## • Unlimited dreams, tap into the potential inside of you.

Today is the day, lay on the sandy beach and it's time to get excited focus on your world of dreams remember nothing comes easy, when you reach out to what it is you like to do, try to overcome all obstacles and eliminate negative actions and find a solution to them, my wife and I have said to our children its always better to dream big, try something

**" Take a risk, you might tip up, by making a few mistakes in life , there will be times when you want to cry and laugh at the mistakes you make ,but you can always be brave and learn from them".**

While revaluing in your potential of big dreams take time and reminisce and appreciate your family and closest friends,

### "Your family give  unlimited love in good times in bad times"

there will be times when you have doubts about your big dream, you will need them to be walking with you on the long and winding road to success, family and friends will be your rock and pillars and strong foundation, family and friends will comfort you in times of hardship and in times of victory, when others will evade you, and not believe in you, others will not be there.
Be loving and humble, treat others with respect, the way you want to be respected.
Sometimes we feel life is too hard or our potential to be great seems like and endless path and journey is seems so far away but that's just our emotions and feeling coming into play. Its ok we are allowed to scream and shout, laugh and cry, find a quiet place to reflex on a quite sunny day things may not go well all time but always remember our life is better than it seems.
Always believe in the power of the Big Dream and the unlimited potential you have

When your life seems overcast foggy, rocky, storms, will decline and you will shine grab your time in the sun. And there will be many times in one's life, you think there is no such thing as hope ,and you are defeated, but don't forget to count the many victories you've won.

# Unlimited dreams, tap into the potential inside of you

"We have more blessings in our lives happen, than defeats."

I have many mistakes that I can't change now, but what I have learnt from the lessons
and misfortunes I have encountered, I give thanks and gratitude for luck to pass me by.
The amount of hours and time I have spent writing, winner's circle of dreams, "it felt like solitude was my only friend" that I can't deny, it can be sometimes a lonely journey heading on the road to success, but I also know

**"My family have up lifted me with their love and great smiles to help me to believe in the dream when I needed it"**

Can I be honest with you, I know you have unlimited potential in you, that you would like to bring out of you, from past experience ,there are something's in life that go to plan and plans that didn't seem to work out right, as I have told you in the book

**"If your dream didn't turn out the way you wanted it to be, always remember you can always dream another dream ,remember your lifeline is full and holds an endless shopping list supply of untapped unlimited potential, don't give up ,try choose another one to explore until you find what's right for you"**

It's so true, I can honestly say, you do have the ability to attain whatever you seek; within you is every potential you can imagine. Give it your best never let it rest; aim higher than you can reach. Give your untapped potential ago; you got nothing, to lose so often, you'll discover that when your talents are set free by your creativity and imagination, you have the capacity to achieve any goal. I have close friends and mentors who can offer their

# Unlimited dreams, tap into the potential inside of you

feedback, help or wisdom, accept the gratitude, ask any successful person who had a dream; they didn't do it on their own.

You can learn much from those who have taken the steps to become the success they are today, don't be afraid or hesitant to step off the accepted path and head off in your own direction, if your heart instinct tells you ,that is the right way for you to go.

**"Always believe that you will ultimately succeed at whatever you do, and never forget the value of persistence, discipline, and determination. You are meant to be whatever you dream of becoming, please don't let others hold you back, find your uniqueness' and your shining light"**

There are times when you must stand alone be brave confident have courage enough within yourself to follow your own dreams, you must be willing to make sacrifices, and capable of changing and rearranging your priorities so that your final goal can be achieved.
Sometimes we need to challenge our comfort zone, it not always the best
there will be times in your life when you must take a few extra risks and stretch out of comfort zone of failure and fear to grow and create your own realities

"You will find the strength and courage to pursue a better and meaning full life, your unlimited potential is inside of you and is waiting to be unveiled to the world and when that happens the confident you possess will show that, it is not enough that you just won't settle for $2^{nd}$ best or any compromise just to get by".

Appreciate yourself by allowing yourself the opportunities to grow, develop, and find your true sense of purpose in this life. The other day I was out running and I was following my own shadow for 9km, it was my shadow that convinced me to carry on and finish my run, but I try not to stand in the shadow of someone

# Unlimited dreams, tap into the potential inside of you

Else, when I know I have my own shining light that leads to inspire to influence,

**A winner's mentality fuelled by action:** "You can dream as long as you believe it can be done"- **Napoleon Hill**

No matter how many times you fall down in your life it matters how you rise up and get back up again you are the winner

# CHAPTER 7 NOTES

# Chapter 8

- ## **No worries, people will think you're crazy.**

"So what if people think you are crazy and creepy or freaky or different I know, I hear it all the time from all walks of life, what's new, join the winners circle of dreams club, why, its fun, enjoy life and go and do something crazy, its better than being boring and dull and sitting around doing nothing and complaining all the time or letting people say to you that's impossible".

What do a big dream and being a little bit crazy have in common they both have a tendency to marry each other, because **they both require each other to a take a risk**

That's the trouble today, a lot of people will say things, you shouldn't do that, you can't do this, and you can't do that, you are just plain mad

A couple a months ago I was on YouTube watching a grand Nan from the USA jumped out of a plane at the wonderful ripe old age 86 when she landed all she said

**"I enjoyed the wonderful experience today; Tomorrows its goanna make me get up and go again"**

If there's anything I've learned just watching the video,

it is action just do it live the dream and life you want, sometimes you need to go out of your comfort zone to be a little bit crazy and do something so different , most people have a little bit of craziness in them. Don't go out and hurt yourself, im not talking about that form of crazy, there's a big difference; you can try your hand at something new that's crazy and fuelled with fun

This is what happens when you do something different and get so excited, people will think you are insane or crazy, too unstable and go straight to the judgement thing again, use all the excuses under the sun to stop you from feeling good.

# No worries, people will think you're crazy.

Why because

**"They people, see you working hard on your dream and achieving it, you have hit their hot spot, where they haven't got any dreams and goals going at all, and they are thinking about all the fear and failures they have had with their dreams and goals and have found their experience just too hard, that they just want to carry on and be average and have a normal and boring life, people will tarnish you and stop you from achieving the dream".**

I do believe we have to be accountable for our own actions and listen to what we are saying to ourselves. The trouble for some of us is accepting that ugly side of us and letting it come out.  people mind power and way of thinking can suppress their inner desires to reach their dreams because they are concerned about what others might think or they don't think they "should" do them. As long as you are ok with "what is you want to do from your heart" and is what you want to do, and you a have plan of action you should go for it. Be proud of who you are

I would never suggest to everybody jumping out of a plane is for everybody, doing anything like that, I guess she had the guts ,reason desire and passion, you can't fault her heart,  think about it who was going to tell her, no you can't jump out of a plane , because you are too old, you or me, I know my answer, it's like someone telling me what colour my daughters hair should be, But when it comes right down to it, some of the most amazing things dreams, goals ,climb mountains, bungee jump, fall from the sky skateboard at 60 years, do all those exciting things in life while your living and not dead, life is too short, you can do it, there's nothing wrong with a little bit of craziness.

# No worries, people will think you're crazy.

Here are 5 powerful keynote Crazy tips.

**1** It's the morning, wake up, get up, sit up, it's the Best time to get crazy and have a clear refreshed mind to do something really special.

**2** When people say you can't do that, use what they said to your advantage, rise up and it will give the incentive to get crazy to just do it.

**3** Use your instinct and inspiration and capitalize on your crazy successful thoughts.

**4** Leaving your job and going into business for yourself might not be so bad after all; you have just come up with a crazy idea and opportunity of buying a successful franchise.

**5** Try your hand at something new that's crazy and fuelled with fun; it's worth its living for.

**A winner's mentality fuelled by action:** "If you don't go after what it is you want, you will never have it, if you don't ask, the answer will be "No". If you don't do something crazy and step outside the box you will also be in the same place"- **Nora Roberts**

No matter how many times you fall down, it matters how you rise up and get back up again you are the winner.

- **The journey commits to your dream it worth it.**

Have you ever ask any great grandparent, grandparents, parents, defector, same sex, who have been married or living together for so many years what's their secret to success, they will tell you in one sentence, it is called responsible, obligation, love and commitment, have you ever read about great successful companies and their longevity at staying at the top of their game for such long time, it's called responsible, obligation, commitment

**"Commit to your dream its worth it, the trouble with most people is lack of it"**

If you want to follow your big dream, you have committed to the dream and it's not easy. The big dream, doesn't happen overnight, it is a long and arduous journey full of excitement, sadness and pain sweet and tears, and many obstacles to overcome, if you commit to your dream long enough to where it is you are going you will Win, writing this book and gathering all the information involved has taken a lot of hard work and I have stuck to the commitment. Publishing the book the winner's circle of dreams will be the ultimate dream, but still is a very tiny successful moment compared to the time I have spent on my journey, it will be a wonderful moment I will cherish, but life still goes on. Focusing on that single moment makes you impatient, till you get there and victorious ,once you've get there, I won't know the smell of sweet success until I have finished completing and writing the book .You see to many people give up the ghost ,a true commitment is a real commitment ,a commitment by heart, which there is no turning back  I know for me there are times when you want to give up on your commitment, because I struggle to come to terms still of restless nights of doubt thinking and stress, and living in either my the future or the past I will talk about the past later on in this book. My success I can share right now is I plod along on my journey Commit to my dream; experiencing every step I take and celebrating small and big achievements.

# The journey commits to your dream it worth it.

I learnt to take advice from my mum and dad about how to be committed ,they told me if you want to do something for somebody you have to show a bit of commitment if you said you were going to mow the lawns for Mr cannon down the road then you need to show commitment and turn up on his door step and you will get paid, so son it's like my job I have to commit to the job or we don't eat , taking advice from others is all good as long it is the right advice to help you to stay committed.

**Mum and dad were the rock and pillars of our family when it came to giving advice; it was for a good reason,**

My mum and dad were married for 45 yrs. I believe commitment shows how powerful it can be, I have always wondered how great couples stay together and ask myself is there a secret to their commitment, taking responsibility, love and family was all that mattered most , In today's world couples today are lucky to last 5yrs to 10yrs, I don't want to blame anyone or offend anyone just because their marriage didn't work out, only they know what has happened, but I look at my parents and how they worked together as a team and for each other and fixed the problems , this was their commitment. Today Angela I have been married for 26 years, there have been times of hardship and it hasn't been all plane sailing but yet we are committed

**"Marriage is like a business, business will go through the good and tuff times it those businesses and marriages that commit and fix problems and endure, are the ones who see and benefit life's rewards" CD Walden**

I care about the people we love that our first instinct is to steer them away from any potential source of suffering. If we commit to anything in life there is that price to pay difficult situations, money problems , death , drugs ,gambling, the more we put strategies in place and overcome and commit the more stronger we get . We must also remember there is no safe passage for commitment, commitment can be here today and travel somewhere else tomorrow.

# The journey commits to your dream it worth it.

**A winner's mentality fuelled by action** "To make a commitment stay, you have to have a big dream, desire and a reason, for commitment to want to stay. Let's start loving ourselves take responsibility find out what we are really capable of instead reflecting on our inner fear"- **CD Walden**

When we make a commitment to a dream, it wasn't about our past but a commitment to go forward in the future because commitment holds the key to our future. I see I am not the only one alone on my journey, everybody is on a journey of commitment; everybody has dreams to commit too, even if we sometimes forget them.

**"Family who love you so much in your life will offer all the support you need, the moment you ask".**

Get committed today and enjoy living the dream you have always dreamed about and you will be the winner.

Here are 12 keynote tips to commit to the dream
1 Make Decision.
2 Paint a picture, Visualize your dream in the future, and how you see it.
3 You need a reason, burning desire.
4 Turn that dream into a goal.
5 Get a plan.
6 Write the commitments down.
7 Split your dreams and goals into short, medium, long term, they need a time line
8 It needs to activated and actioned.
9 Measure your progress you are making
10 Research your dream and find out exactly what it is you really want
11 Get enthusiastic , excited, be confident, positive, start living, winning, and endure to the end
12 Eliminate all negativity

No matter how many times you fall down in your life it matters how you rise up and get back up again you are the winner.

## • Let Courage lead you closer to dream.

I hope and pray since you have been reading the stories in this book that they have been inspiring for you, to dream the big dream.

I was so excited recently, I talked about commitment, you are the winner, if it has helped you to move closer and forward and take another step towards your journey

**"Truthfully I am so happy for you". Craig Walden**

I said that many people today that don't want to make that commitment to a big dream; they sell themselves short, because they lack courage of one's self.

I can tell you today if you have committed to the dream and things are going to plan you are ever so close to achieving what it is you will achieve

**One Question I have to ask from you**

**"Do you still have the courage and determination and discipline to continue on to pursue your dream", if you said yes, then you are the true champion".**

Courage and determination and self-discipline are so important because they give you that extra sense of hope that will help you across the finish line

My friend once said the journey on the road to success can be a lonely one.

Before I made a trek towards that road, my friend said you need equip yourself with the right toolkit for the unknown, be prepared and **"beware of how to overcome trails of adversity",** boy he was so right, nothing comes easy

Craig Get excited you must have courage and determination and discipline to get through life experiences that will be heading your way, you will be heading down a new path of new adventures, you will notice the changes a new day and a new challenge.

# Let Courage lead you closer to dream.

Have you ever had, family, friends or people helped you in times of need .thank you for the words of encouragement. **We all need a hand with something that we need to deal with.**

I also found courage through times, of adversity that have tested me in my life to great lengths. Here are two true stories of courage.

1 Have you experienced heartache and pain at losing love ones, whether it be through war ,sickness, natural circumstances maybe you could be grieving right now, or you know of someone, this has recently happened to.

this is a subject that people find hard to come to terms with, for some the grieving and emotional, traumatic processes stay in embedded in their hearts for a very long time, I have lost my mum, dad, 2 brothers 2 sisters I miss them so much and believe that one day I will see them again, we all will cry for the moments, we will always remember the love they gave to us that will be in our hearts forever. Mum and dad said to me remember if you have a dream you must have the courage to do it and don't stop.

**"Life is so short".**
It felt life had taken everything away from me, especially those who are very close to you, more recently in Jan 2012 my big sister Lorraine whom I love so dearly passed away, I remember every time I got the chance to see her when I was in Hamilton, I would make time with her , I don't recognize the pain and suffering she went through in her last days ,for me it's the memories and what she gave to me throughout her life time, that taught me to grow into the person I am today. **If I sit around and swell in the past, I am defeating my own purpose of success**, I can hear my mum and dad and my big brothers and sister saying don't give up courage is in you, get back up again keep going and don't stop what you started keep believing your destiny and the dream.

# Let Courage lead you closer to dream.

**One of the reasons why courage is so powerful is**

**"What fuels me up at this moment, is to get up each and every morning, and say today's a great day, I am getting closer to my dream, I am going to finish the book winners circle of dreams the milestone, I am so thankful what they, each and everyone of my own family, my wife and children have done for me, over the years, most of all I am true to me".**

I don't know what my mum and dads and brothers and sisters future dreams were, one thing is they give me the belief, love courage and inspiration, whatever I do, how I become successful in my life, my love ones will be there to walk with me in spirit

Back in early 2003 I was working as a night shift manger working in at a supermarket called big fresh, work was from 4pm in the afternoon till 3am next day , one early morning I came home from work , noticed I was breathing heavy, my wife said to me hey Craig are you ok and I said not really, I looked tired and withdrawn, she booked me in to see the doctor , that day the doctor said I had an irregular heartbeat so called heart murmur ,straight away they sent me to see the cardiologist at Tauranga hospital for tests , I had never been to the hospital in my whole entire life ,always played sport and loved the great out doors

**"That day the shock of my life was about to unfold, the cardiologist told me I had an enlarged heart and that I had 16 month 18 months to live, if I didn't do anything about my heart I would die."**

Apparently I had rheumatic fever when I was eight years old, a virus had destroyed one of my heart valves and wasn't functioning and pumping the blood around the body properly causing my heart to be enlarged.

# Let Courage lead you closer to dream.

For the first time in my life I was scared, I looked good on the outside but bad on the inside

**"My mind was fuelled with fear, have you ever seen a grown man cry, I wept and wept and wept, I went from invincible to vulnerable and from a confident strong man to a very week mouse".**

The doctor said goes home and think it over, and prepare you for the operation. For a couple of weeks I pondered over all the worst thing s that could happen, the thought of the smell of death was knocking at my door and I was feeling so down and out, in a rut and black hole, going into a state of depression, there had been times I was over obsessed mentally with bitterness, I was blaming everyone I loved, for my unfortunate dilemma. Until one day

My wife and children triggered me out of darkness and turned around to me and said dad you need to think positively, and think about getting stronger, we need you

"Don't give up have the courage to fight"

There are so many family happy times ahead in the future to come, my daughter said to me dad you got to be around at my 21$^{st}$ and my wedding, dad you got to have the operation do it for us, we love you dad, my family had bought me back into the light, I didn't want to die, **they had given me the courage to get up and live again**. I should be grateful for our families who give us the courage to magnify our love and strengths. On Feb. 1$^{st}$ 2003 I was admitted to Waikato hospital I remember the evening so clearly it was an experience of a life time I will never forget, a young man from Tokoroa was crying next to me, because he had to have a triple valve operation, and here was me thinking and worried about my one valve, he lived and played rep rugby was targeted for chiefs development squad it was his life ,and his big dream, his dad gave him a golf book to read and said when you get out of hospital, try golf it something new.

## Let Courage lead you closer to your dream.

Being in hospital taught me something as well,

**"You may think your dreams are over, just because you are at a crossroads of your life but you can always do something new, and if you think you are in bad shape there are worst cases patients in hospital who don't have the option to live and breathe and dream another day, that night hope and courage stood out like a light house and come to the rescue and gave comfort to both of us".**

So that evening I called all of my family and said I love you one more time, The next morning I headed to surgery ,the operation would last for 5 hours, my doctor and surgeon was from the Philippines ,he gave me reassurances things were going to be fine ,I found the courage to speak to him ,my last words to him were , "doctor god has blessed you, he had given you the courage to use your gifted surgical hands to help people get better and lead a long and prosperous life  my heart operation was a success,  it was an act of courage and a battle to believe and get back up again

Everyone on this earth will experience trauma, death, financial, critic, sickness, and doubt, Sadness failure fear darkness and despair many obstacles at some stage in their lives, but we have a choice to overcome these with change of mind-set courage and determination, and replace it with hope .love, big dreams, strategies victory, and opportunities.

Over the past 35 years, I've had to deal with these events in my life. Believe me, it's been a long struggle.

But no matter what comes my way, I still find the courage to continue. Courage and hope have been really powerful in the pursuit of my dreams. Even though it can be hard, courage has kept me on the right path

Courage is about if we fall down, it how we get up again, many successful people have fallen down and got back up again. To become successful

# Let Courage lead you closer to your dream.

"Whatever challenges you face right now, you have the power to make two choices 1 whether to let the world affect you in a crazy way 2 or stamp your dreams on the world".

 I found out the hard way to blame others for my mistakes and the mishaps and yet I couldn't blame myself for the truths that needed mending in my life
you will never be able to have your dream job nor live your dream life unless you first step outside your comfort zone, find the courage to dream big enough to identify what it is. Dream big with a clear vision for your future life, start telling yourself it's going to be bigger and brighter than your pasts, to overcome the setbacks and failures that present themselves on the way to your goals is what brings the greatest joy of achievement. You must have guts courage will power determination to stay on the right path  **"It is through perseverance in the face of adversity that the big dreams start of ordinary and become extra-ordinary you are the winner"**

Here are 7 Keynote Winners circle of dreams courage tips
1 Use your Courage to overcome fear, you will win
2 Use your Courage to overcome your past, you will win
3 Use your Courage to forgive, you will win
4 Use your Courage to love, you will win
5 Use your Courage to step up a level, you will win
6 Use your Courage to be a mentor and a leader, you will win
7 Use your Courage to action, dream big, plan and start something new, you will win

 **<u>A winners mentality fuelled by action</u>:** "To become a champion, you have to believe in yourself, when nobody else will – **Sugar Ray Robinson**

No matter how many times you fall down in your life it matters how you rise up and get back up again you are the winner.

- **Don't let the past hold u back.**

Courage is everything when you have to let your past go

**"How many of us are prepared to let the past go. If you are holding on to issues of the past let them go, it will be well worth it for you".**

Have you ever taken a look around your city lately to see all the new landscape and buildings going up all around you, you will notice, there is pretty much a balance of old building of the past and new, most cities look at expansion for the future, even though you see old buildings about, the city has replicas and stories to tell of the past, but doesn't stay in the past. The other night I was listening to all of my old music on my mp3 and then I started to think about the past, and memories of those good old days, 'you know what' I had just realized, I was conditioned and trapped in my past. I ask myself this question was that a good thing or a bad thing. you see I always thought of my life currently could hide behind my music and living the past will fix my present problems I know now, the past doesn't have any bearing on the actions I take and my success in the future.

As for me I am prepared to about lay down those past skeletons in the closet and get excited about the future

**"Many people stay trapped in their past and are fearful of the future".**

You see when I get lost in my music it takes me back to the past both, good and some bad, what I am trying to say to you is we can tend to dwell in the how things use to be and spend the whole time talking about how hard things can be instead of carving out happy life for our future. We can take a look at our past learn from it and not get stuck in it.

## Don't let the past hold u back

"For some people, the past is like mind-set prison, you are under lock and key and there is no way out of the mind-set prison. You see, you believe you don't have freedom to do the things you want to do, and the obstacle called the past stops you from achieving your goals in life. It is your thoughts that put a restriction, negativity hurt and fear into your body mind-set and soul".

This is a true story about a man I know who had been through a painful life experience ,health death of close family and the hurt of losing everything he had, it had taken the man along time about 5 years to let the past go, he said he was an enemy to people , he was so upset that he blamed everyone for his misfortune, he was so entrenched with battle scars in the past he couldn't get out of it in 1989 this man and his wife bought his first house, in 2000 he and his wife bought his second house ,in 2007 life was going great, this man had a wonderful home, wife and family and had just sent his daughter of to university, the man always had a dream to look at the future and was a very proud person. One day this man saw an article in the newspaper to buy a business, the man made an inquiry, he had met this group of business people, he had good faith in and trust, the business was a franchise for financial brokerage worth 50,000 he and his wife went to the lawyer got all the paper work done and bought the franchise. As well as that he bought a car worth 22,000 for the business, also the man had paid out 38,000 for an overseas business venture the man was holding down two jobs to pay off the mortgage feed the family and pay for the business loans.

The first couple of weeks were great, the business advisors, were great, everything seem to be working out smoothly they would call regularly, but little did he know that, This man's life was about to be turned upside down, all he and his wife had worked so hard for was gone.

## Don't let the past hold u back.

**"May of 2007 was a disaster the franchise office was closed and all the furniture and office equipment had vanished and the overseas investors were nowhere to be seen. The man had borrow loans from second tier lenders and put up collateral on his house"**

The man and his wife had been landed a bombshell, 2007 would be best remembered as financial nightmare this man and his family would never ever forget, and the pain was so rooted deep down with in his heart for so many years to come.

The receivers called in the bank mortgage on the house and his kids watched in despair as the debt collectors repossessed the family car all of their life savings gone

This man plight has taken him so many years to change; he has excepted that what happened in the past can be at times hurtful but he knows you cannot change the past and what has happen, he told me learning about the past experience has made him more aware of making good strong financial decisions for the future and what to watch for he is so grateful for his wife and family to stand beside him, he also said, this did happen to me yesterday I may have learnt a big lesson about risk as well and I paid the price, it happened seeing as there is no way to travel back in time, there is no way to change the past

**"I have moved on, it's about the future and not the past, those things that went wrong I can't make them right they are gone, it's all about focus and the future. I have accepted my mistakes/failures and moved on from times gone by I am excited much better equipped to control my bright future said the man".**

# Don't let the past hold u back.

**Questions you may ask yourself**
1 I would like to leave the past behind?
2 How can I do this?
3 What's does my exciting future have install for me?

Here are 10 powerful Keynote winners circle of dreams tips to leave your past behind.
1 Prey for believing, faith, healing
2 Drop your past before you seek the future.
3 Deal with past issues but don't make them an everyday habit
4 Mistakes made in the past don't have to be made in the future
5 Mr Future, I will introduce to you Mr Past & Mr Negativity who are your enemy
6 Dwelling on the past issues too much, can be a fruitless pursuit; it will take more energy out of you.

7 Today you can control your present, future, yesterday past is dead and buried

8 Don't kick yourself and take the rap for peoples past actions and events that were out of your control. The only one hurting themselves is you

9 Its your choice, a past fuelled with darkness or a future fuelled with light

10 When you have finished with your past write down your strategies goals and dreams to see you have a bright future.

**A winner's mentality fuelled by action** "People will always blame their past for circumstances for what & where they are, I don't believe in circumstances, those people who get on in this world, are people who get up and look for circumstances they want, if they can't find them, make them – **George Bernard Shaw**

No matter how many times you fall down in your life it matters how you rise up and get back up again you are the winner.

- **Need advice you a need coach.**

So you still want to pursue your big dreams and you are stuck in a rut, you don't know who to turn too, and you feel like you want to quit, take charge of those emotions, 'solution solved'.

"We need to ask for help".

But what do we do , instead of getting excited about your dream, your dream turns into a nasty dream of worry and heartache , we all do it, **we try to go it, alone in life**, I've tried hard and things never seem to work, and then you finally want to give up in life , human instinct has it, we want to do everything on our own , that's great to ,but its ok if we ask for a helping hand, our families and friends can be good as well ,and sometimes not for various reasons, great families will leave a mark to influence and not to destroy, coaches can do the same thing inspire and influence for a life time no matter how big your dreams are, and the situation you are in

**"A coach will have the ability to influence a person's life for the better and uncover and develop the abilities and talents that lie within you".**

Ask yourself this question 1 when we were babies who helped us? Who was our coach? "Mum and dad" when we were at school, polytec, university who was our coach? "Your teacher or counsellor", when we get the flu who is our coach? "Your doctor, if our car needs repairs, who is our coach? "Your mechanic" you are looking for spiritual, advice, marriage guidance, who is your coach your minister, priest, pastor. You played sport both national and locally, who is our coach, "your team coach"

**"The purpose role of a coach is to advise, and who help people with problems, decisions, and goal attainment in daily life, help keep you FOCUSED on the right path and to become that better person"**

# Need advice you a need coach.

Top Sports people, performers, successful writer's, speakers, successful companies and businesses have one thing in common they have a business mentor and a coach to advise them and help them to get to a better performance level .

**<u>A winner's mentality fuelled by action:</u>** "If you want your dream to become a reality and taken to another level a coach and a mentor can take you to a higher dimension". **CD Walden**

I have a friend who is in the fitness industry as a trainer who advises his clients and myself to transform from unfit to, how to stay in shape, exercise, eat healthy and stay in top peak condition at the top of their career, you can't do it on your own, you need a helping hand from others that know more about fitness than you know, good information with great action regular visits to the gym and diet, monitored performance gets nothing but the best results for my clients.

A friend of mine told me his coach has the team practice 8 times a week to get all aspects of their passing, tackling defensive, attacking skill sets right practice, practice, practice. Listen and learn to be coachable is the key to winning this season.

Maybe you have been challenged with obstacles at times, thinking I was never going to make it or finish winner's circle of dreams their have been days that it felt like it

Its is so satisfying for me to know,

**"I have several coaches to help inspire me and influence me and lift me up and say don't quit I am so thankful for their thoughts and words of powerful, encouragement, I can ring my coaches and keep in contact with them via email, they believe that what I am doing is right, they are always their for me."**

# Need advice you a need coach.

Maybe you have a dream right know ,take it to the next level find a great coach and a mentor who will help you, listen to what they say to get you closer to your target,

Try Source out different coaches or mentors that can help strengthen you in different areas of your life physical financial spiritual educational, mental to help you achieve your dream.

Truly don't try going it on your own, the experience I have had in my life ,I paid a hefty price, it pays to seek out the right information and get the right advice, mistakes can be costly to you and your family business ,performance, sport, company or small business ,you may a have a dream ,but still it takes wining coach and mentor  a written plan with the great advice to eliminate risk.

"Find that coach who will have your best interest at heart".

Here are 6 Key winners circle of dream tips how to find the right coach

1 Who can I tell?
2 Do I know them enough to trust them?
3 Can I tell my coach about my strengths and weaknesses?
4 Does my coach lead by example?
5 Will my coach hold me accountable in stormy weather?
6 Have I found the right coach to say to me personally don't quit?
**A winner's mentality fuelled by action:** "We all need the best strategies to execute dreams – **Azim Premji**

No matter how many times you fall down in your life it matters how you rise up and get back up again you are the winner.

- ## **Time waits for no one, not even dreamers.**

These are Mick Jagger's famous words Time waits for no one and cause it won't wait for me.

Don't wait for missed dreams and opportunities.

### **TICK.TOCK.TICK. TOCK**

These are the words of rolling stone singer Mick jagger, time waits for no one it won't wait for me, that's is so true and the same goes with dreams do something and work alongside of time .let time be your partner and friend and build a long lasting relationship together with one and other because if you reach the full potential of your dreams and turn them into reality you will reap the benefits & rewards

Haven't sorted out where your dreams are heading yet

Don't stress, don't worry, be happy, just have fun

Just remember to love yourself, and get excited when you are on the journey of dreams I am here to help you to help your self

My Question is, "**are you doing the one thing, you love doing most, right now**"?

Maybe you are still pondering over what it is still you would like to do

Or maybe you don't want to do anything at all at this point, but it's ok.

## Time waits for no one, not even dreamers.

There are 3 things in life that set us all a part 1- **Time** 2- **Choices** 3- **Free agency**.

**"Everybody has no excuse not to dream and achieve the things that they have always wanted to do in their lives because we all have 24 hours in a day and 365 days to be successful".**

I say don't wait for the new year's resolution, the time could be and should be now.

As far as choices go, it is up to you to make choices, I can't make a choice for you and I won't, good ones, bad ones and it's all about experience and growth, if you want to dream dreams, you will have to make a choice about which dream you are going to make into a reality.

For the majority of people ,our dreams are locked away in the cupboard, or is too far away and untouchable , or Its sounds like something that's bad and ,we all want to put into the too hard basket or sweep it under the carpet for a rainy day .

We all blame ourselves, for not being responsible, for not organising our time, procrastinating about the things we should have been done today, and not put them off until tomorrow.

I myself have missed out on to many opportunities in my life time and yet we all get one chance to make something of our short lives we have on this planet, but I am not going to stand around and wait for time to go by "are you". We are born to win

Ask yourself this question, who didn't Dream? But what did we do with our time?

You see we all do it, as human beings to little kids through adult hood until the day we part from this world. You see Time waits for no one; it keeps going forward and not backwards.

## Time waits for no one, not even dreamers.

"We can't stop time; it's our existence here on earth that determines time and what we have chosen to do with that allocated time".

Good time
Bad time
Clocks ticking
You see Time waits for no one,
Here are 7 key winners circle of dreams tips, about how you use your time

1 What am I doing with my time right now?

2 Is my time productive or unproductive?

3 Procrastination is a killer of time, don't put of things tomorrow, and get them done now.

4 Let time be a partner and friend working together and not your enemy

5 Organise your time.

6 Everyone has 24 hours in a day, it what you do with it, that's matters most.

7 If I use time to my advantage will I be successful.

In the words of the late George Harrison Ex Beatles.
 This his story about **time**

"It's being here now that's important. There's no past and there's no future. Time is a very misleading thing. All there is ever, is the now. We can gain experience from the past, but we can't relive it; and we can hope for the future, but we don't know if there is one."
— **George Harrison**

No matter how many times you fall down in your life it matters how you raise up and get back up again you are the winner.

## • Time and Momentum.

Time and Momentum will propel you into the future.
It's so important to use your time; do momentums checks of your dreams and goals today, where do you want to go? if you don't , you could end up sliding backwards
In my book I talk about When I was a kid growing up in the late 1960s early 1970s **I loved setting up dominos** with my brothers and sisters , the cool thing about domino s ,was watching the them follow and fall down one after another.
Dreams and Goals and Targets produce the same effect, 1 falls down, 1 follows.

Momentum helps you achieve what's possible and becomes the key to winning and losing in life, without time momentum and drive to push you forward you will be sliding backwards.

**"This is how to create momentum and success in such a short time, sit up and get up, put your jogging shoes on, just do it, How to use your time effectively ,the  1$^{st}$ hour is the most important time of any given day, it gives you clarity and set the tone for rest of the day.**
**Once in motion for the day you are more likely to stay in motion and continue on".**

Your personal life is the same, time with momentum, is when you are meeting your dreams goals and targets, one after another. Then your life starts to get exciting knowing you have achieved 1 goal 2 goal 3 goal and so on.

<u>**A winner's mentality fuelled by action**</u>" Success comes from taking the initiative and following up... persisting... eloquently expressing the depth of your love. What simple action could you take today to produce a new momentum toward success in your life"? **- Toney Robbins**

No matter how many times you fall down in your life it matters how you rise up and get back up again you are the winner.

# CHAPTER 8 NOTES

# Chapter 9

## • Its easy to focus on the outcome, start winning first to give you a chance.

Life as we all know it is fuelled with,

**1** time and the choice, what we will do with it,

**2** times will give us a beginning **3** time will be the judge and jury to give an ending, to the things we have achieved in our life time here on earth.

Talking and writing about time has really questioned me, I know now if I am to win and achieve the big dream, what it is I want in life

**"I have to organise my time and action my time, to generate a productive way to go forward in my life and achieve winning results".**

You see so many people say they would like to achieve something great in their lives, they know what the outcome and possibilities are,

Big dreamers and top achievers use the **AAA formula Action-Activate-Activity,** to help them get what it is they want to achieve , they start at the start line and begin to take small, medium, and giant steps to move forward at all times. The day I see a marathon runner and basketball player win a race or win a game from the side line will be amazing.

Successful people in life already have planned what the next set of strategies are, and have another goal immediately in mind. When you want to dream big and you have that burning desire and passion ,and happiness inside of you , you either have it or you don't , these things are by instinct , where ever I speak or if you are reading the book winners circle of dreams , I can't make you do anything you want to do , I can't put the desire passion or happiness inside of you ,this has to come from you , getting back to the outcome ,yes it is nice to know what the end result may feel like ,

## It's easy to focus on the outcome, start winning first to give yourself a chance.

but it will always be just another wish, and a waste of precious time

**"The only way to find out how good we will be and how our outcome will turn out is to challenge our outcome head on as human beings, begin our quest and journey, action, and get our hands dirty"**

I want this so badly , anything is possible to do what I want , if I don't start at all ,there will be no end result at all , great successful people never quit , along the way find solutions to **overcome** to **outcomes**. So if you are reading this book right now and you have got to this point you are capable and ready to move on and conquer all that you desire,

"I never dreamed it could be possible to be an author and speaker, but with the persistence courage and action to stay on that long and winding road to success has been an experience, one I will never forget, I kept telling myself I have an obligation and responsibilities to stick it and endure to the end, you see when you start your dream and see it through to the end, and you become successful **"you find out who the true you is" CD Walden**

Finding out the true you is in direct opposition to staying in your comfort zone. When you have stretched out a little each time from your normal life you would have experienced a stronger and fulfilling life for the better, I mention the ant in my book they are a wonderful creature, who are persistent , vibrant and reliable, and what that means is, whatever the environment, ants never stagnate and never quit, always collecting their harvest , they are always busy helping improve , build a colony wall within solid structural inner and outer foundations necessary to keep empire thriving efficiently and effectively.

## It's easy to focus on the outcome, start winning first to give yourself a chance.

So today don't wait another moment Give yourself a real chance to do what you want to do, please take action today I recommend you do it for you,

**"Leave a legacy do something, go from ordinary too good to great to something extraordinary, you will not only change your vision and life but also inspire to influence friends and family".**

Those big dreamers and top Fortune 500 companies and people who followed their own instincts led us in new directions carved their names into the history books.

Please remember when you dream big , as I did ,not all went my way , but I can surely count the many blessings on my fingers, what I have had go my way , what hasn't or didn't go your way , look at the experience you have gained from it ,which lead us to into knew territories ,and for a good reason. Keep doing what you keep doing and get the same result, I say and that's called insanity; always remember as humans we try things to build up experience and stamina to prepare us, to be better people or to prepare us for something bigger.

**"Everybody has a gift to do something special our life, dreams and goals aren't given to us on a candy stick".**

**"Tom hanks once said in the movie Forrest Gump, life is like a box of chocolates you don't know what you going to get".**

**Many people in life are waiting for something great to happen, and will be waiting around for a life time".**

Successful people are willing to make it happen .if you are thinking about what it is you would like to do, don't be scared of fear, try something and just do it, whatever you do in life there is always a price to pay, you do nothing and get nothing, or take that risk, you will try something for that greater chance of winning for you.

# Its easy focus on the outcome, start winning first to give you a chance.

"Question, have you walked the same foot path every day, most of your life? Do you go to work every day doing the same boring job"?

Don't miss out on the opportunities' that are in front of you

Life is full of so much excitement, adventure, new frontiers, surprises and you don't know what rewards you will receive if you don't make a choice and try.

Here are 5 keynote powerful winners circle of dreams tips

**1** Decide what you want.
**2** Write down your strategy, activation, activity and action plan
**3** Organise your time
**4** Proceed to the start line
**5** Go forward and make small- medium- long term things happen today and in the future.

**A winner's mentality fuelled by action**
"No matter what happens, always be yourself."
"Our thoughts make us what we are."
"Nothing can bring you peace but yourself."
**- Dale Carnegie**


No matter how many times you fall down in your life it matters how you rise up and get back up again you are the winner.

- **You must start with a process and performance plan today, to see the outcome**

Are you at the stage, where you are ready to make a decision today? Do you have that big idea and dream in mind yet? Or are you still at the crossroads to say this looks hard? Be honest have you got a plan? Would you be willing to set goals How's your time and organisation going, don't worry you are not alone, there are many people who are out in the big wide world who,

1 Don't want to know.
2 Do know but don't care
3 Don't like goal setting.

Remember what I said in my book, I talked about how to overcome obstacles of a dreaded dream or goal, you don't have to live in self-doubt, try replacing it with courage and faith, I was in the same place you are at right now.

Be brave, front up making it to starting line and from scratch, believe me when I say this, it is a good thing, and there will be challenges. If you are serious about your future dreams and goals you will need a plan of action to help you and guide you on the journey, listen if you don't have a plan then getting off the ground will be much harder, just like an airplane with no fuel in the tank, it can't take off to reach its destination, you don't have a plan, then maybe that big dream is still just a big wish, do you know difference between a goal and a dream.

The only difference between a goal and a dream is Goals are dreams with time line and deadlines. Plan and dreams and goals will save you time and heartache and mistakes and maybe money depending how big your task is.

# You must start with a process and performance plan today, to see the outcome

Example dreams and goals
1 You may want to lose weight and increase your health
2 You would like to earn more money for your family
3 You would like to go back to school
4 You are looking at new job promotion
5 You may want to build a better relationship
6 You want to build or buy your first home
I start to use a basic simple plan to help me get started, you may already have a plan, and depending on what it is you are trying to achieve, a plan can be changed to apply to your circumstances, start today without hesitation

Here are 5 simple principles to getting started

What-Why-How-Who-When Plan
1 **What** do you want to do, I will make a decision?
2 **Why** do I want to do this, with every dream, goal, task there is also the reason why
3 **How** will I go about putting a process plan together so I will achieve my dream, goal, and task?

4 **Who** can help me or assist me with a plan, information and knowledge

5 **When** will I start and complete my timeframes and deadlines for my dreams, goals, and task.

# You must start with a process and performance plan today, to see the outcome

**Example plan**

**a What** was my dream, to write a book and when finished, publish winner's circle of dreams on Amazon?

**b Why** do I want to do this, my reason to be an author and speaker, meet lots of new people earn good money and help inspire to influence peoples live, Travel the world speaking.

**c How** will I go about putting a process plan together I realize I must write dreams and goals down on paper or in journal, diary, on the fridge and use technology device such as iPod, computer, laptop, cell phone I will write down a list of my 1 short term goals and advance to 2 medium and then 3 long term and then prioritize them with each dream, goal, task broken down with a deadline

**d Who** can help me or assist me with a plan, information and knowledge, I have a business mentor, friends ,family who help encourage me ,who I can call on for advice I will use resources online and read books audios and attend functions and seminars.

**e When** will I start and complete my timeframes and deadlines for my dreams, goals, and task I will write down **start dates** for my dreams and goals and also write down appropriate deadlines next to the dream, goals, task so I know I am committed to those tasks to be finished and completed within the time frame .

# You must start with a process and performance plan today, to see the outcome

## **Timeline**

20 yr goal
10 yr goal
5 yr goal
3 yr goal
1 yr goal
6 month goal
3 month goal
1 month goal
2 week goal
1 week goal
Daily goal

A successful person is always setting new dreams and goals, Goal setting is absolutely critical for you to help you build a blueprint foundation of your desired dreams and goals, if I didn't write down my dreams and goals on paper that I wanted to achieve ,it was always going to be just another hopeless wish.

I remember the day I said I was going to write my book I started to put my dreams and goals down in writing, and on the fridge, every day I keep looking at my dreams and goals, the book has become a commitment and that commitment is what drives me to it.

Keep your dream and goal realistic, and better than your best, but believable and achievable any goal you want in life you got to believe you will get it. If you don't believe in your dreams or goals, you will never go ahead and pay the price for it.

Try to start of with short term goals and with a time frame and deadline, the reason I say this, I love it when I have achieved a short term goal, writing this particular book, I have to had write

# You must start with a process and performance plan today, to see the outcome

and break down the inserts and chapters into short term goals for me it worked quite well, because for me, It felt good that the short

term goal and task was actioned, out of the way, done and dusted so I could move forward and get on to the next goal.

The thing about a short term goal is it achievable usually Instantly gratifying, if you action, but if you put off the task of the short term goal you will definitely, go cold turkey and lose interest Various types of goals can be money financial wealth power, clothes the new car, overseas trips and vacations with family, health and fitness, spiritual, family relationships, marriage. I am a firm believer if you write and place a timeframe down next to your dreams and goals they will get done

As humans we look for goals in all areas of your life because we all need them, just remember there is a need for multiple goals for you

**1** Personal life family, friends,
**2** Physical health
**3** Job, business, financial,
**4** Spiritual wellbeing,
All types of goals are great , you have the will to achieve as many as you want
Some people say that's not possible, well a goal is just one thing there are people out there, that will not achieve any goals at all, because they simply don't want to give up their time, a set of goals in one's life is nothing more than a combination of minor short term, medium long term goals all put together, they are the small things that keep you moving towards the things you want

# You must start with a process and performance plan today, to see the outcome

I get so excited when I achieve my personal dreams and goals, you say to yourself, I think im going to write down a goal today, You get that ,you start to set sail on course for your next adventure, you change and become a new person with new belief and confidence.

I know with each day and every little step I take I set out to finish my book; my dream becomes a step closer to achieving what it is I set out to do and finally becomes reality.

That's why I say to those of you who are reading my book right now I will say it to you again, it very important write your dreams and goals down on paper or in your journal or in your device planner, if you haven't make a start today don't wait for tomorrow

Here are 7 key Winners circle of dreams & goals planning principles

1 Write down your dreams and goals
2 Assign a date next to them
3 If I stay committed and focused towards my dreams and goals, what's in it for me

4 There are obstacles in my life identify them and move them

5 Find a mentor, business coach people in the community group who will help you.

6 Find out about all the information and knowledge you need to know in pursuit of your dreams and goals

7 Be responsible today take a look at how bright your future and life will be in 1 week, 3months, 5yr 20 or 30 years from now.


There are 6 key tips you need to ask yourself about your future.
1 What's your personal accomplishment going to look like?
2 Have you thought about what it is you, want to be someday?
3 What kind of person do you want to be?

## You must start with a process and performance plan today, to see the outcome

**4** What would you want to own?
**5** What do you want to have in life?
**6** It is so easy to set goals, you must take action and use your time wisely, what it is you want, if you don't know what it is you want, how can you possibly get what it is you want

Remember start off with a simple process and performance plan today.

No matter how many times you fall down in your life it matters how you rise up and get back up again you are the winner.

## It's never too late to pick up on your scattered dreams.

Going through all those obstacles in life and being challenged time and time again I can remember my parents telling me never give up on those things you really want to pursue and become I have studied the thought physiology of many successful people, whatever happened in the past is gone, it's about the future and what we do with our time, we have here on earth, and the legacy we leave in turn, becomes our final destiny.

If at first you don't succeed try again, as many great people of our time have said, it is never too late to pick up on your scattered dreams
I visualize the amazing possibilities ahead now and in the future, real soon, publishing my book, and holding it in my hand, it was just that, a scattered dream, that is so close to becoming a reality,

# It's never too late to pick up on your scattered dreams.

to inspire to influence many people all over
Many people need to pick up on their scattered dreams and ignite them again. I remember taking an employment seminar at our church, a few of the men had mentioned about unfinished business in their lives that they needed to take care of.

I ask the men to write down what it was they needed to do, they all had said they had dreams that they have started and never finished. I said well maybe it's time to start on winning back those scattered dreams and working on them again, it's never too late to finish off what it is you started.
Im a believer and we all believe in something, you may have a health problem and you want to get better.

Maybe you did have faith and it was scattered everywhere in life, maybe you had a scattered dream to become that someone you thought was possible, because others said your scattered dream was impossible you stop believing in your dream.

The power of big dreams is its ability, to show us what we are capable of.

A scattered dream simply means you have not yet dreamed the way to get there...
Dream the destination, and then dream the journey and process on how to get there.
Take charge of your scattered dreams; take action today, finish off what it is you started, think about what can be achieved, and what if it is possible.

No matter how many times you fall down in your life it matters how you rise up and get back up again you are the winner.

## • Your Dreams don't have to be complicated.

My farther once said "We try and can lead a simple life", but it's sure not easy and you don't have to the make things in your life complicated. Do those dreams really have to be complicated, stress you out, leave you with no faith and more grey hair at the end of the day, hey how about trying this, write this down on paper, im going to Say <u>simple 4 step formula</u>, **1** <u>what it is I have to say</u>, **2** <u>action what I said I would do</u>, **3** <u>write down and plan how I said I was going to do it</u>, **4** <u>attach a timeline, when I said was going get it done it completed.</u>

I do believe there is light shining at the end of the tunnel and that my journey to publish the book is coming to an end, I am so grateful and thankful I have endured to the end, stuck to the task and are really excited about what the future holds for me and my family . I can honestly say there have been times I just wanted to throw the towel in, and this dream I had, completing and finishing the book was just a wish. There would be times I would lay down and cry because I had no belief in what I was trying to achieve.

We make our dreams in life much harder than it seems ourselves, I have to be honest, you whatever dream you are too pursue in life, you will have **<u>to fight and endure</u>** for what you believe in,

**"Don't stop when you do, that when dreams become complicated and we become enslaved, to doubt, failure, neglect, impossible, those thoughts will start to set in"**.

We as the human race really think at times dreams and life seems complicated, physically, mentally, and spiritually. We have to remind ourselves that our dreams have taken us this far, it time to move forward and not slide backwards, I am born to win.

# Your Dreams don't have to be complicated.

When we were kids growing up I loved playing with a little magnify glass, I would look through the magnify glass the little insects I could see, were bigger than normal, I found out one day it helped me burn paper as well, I won't go there

But have you ever been behind a magnify glass lately. A whole lot of things in life seem bigger than they really are; maybe we magnify our mind and all our problems in the same way and really make those problems bigger than they really are.

Big dreams with problems don't have to be that way, there is always an answer to every dream with a problem, "Say what it is you have to say", "do what it is you said", "how are you going to do what you said" , and "when will you finish what you were going to do" you must be in control and take responsibility of the dream, don't let the dream with the problem take control and responsibility of you, before a dream problem tends to get bigger than they really are, find that solution to it now, and take action today don't wait for tomorrow.

Here are 6 key tips you need to ask yourself
**1** Fight for your dream.
**2** Believe in your dreams.
**3** You stop dreaming, life starts to gets complicated.
**4** Fix the complication with a solution, before it gets bigger than it really is, and gets way out of hand.
**5** Endure and don't stop,
**6** There is a shining light at the end of the tunnel.

<u>**A winner's mentality fuelled by action**</u> "Life is filled with **10%** Complications & **90%** how I react." -**John Maxwell**

No matter how many times you fall down in your life it matters how you rise up and get back up again you are the winner

- **How to become a conqueror of fear and negativity.**

I have had people say to me Craig, I have a bad past, something's just didn't go right, my sports team just aint performing in the areas when it counts, I had a bad marriage, relationship or that business went down the tube, I didn't achieve my big dream, I do listen, but most people talk up fear and negativity like it's the most fashionable popular thing to do in their daily lives, you don't have to become the slave, it doesn't have to be that way.

When we give in to our fears and negativity, we miss out countless opportunities to grow. Become the warrior, you know you are, and not a worrier, I say to you , if you will confront your fears and negativity today ,you will change for the better ,and be blessed with a brighter tomorrow .

Become a master of your own destiny, and not a slave, to your fears, negativity replace them, with faith & courage and good thoughts, your confidence will grow stronger and stronger, and you will conquer negativity and fear today

You have nothing to lose and everything to gain, start believing in what's possible instead of what's not possible

start asking questions like "What if I achieve my dreams, its going to change my whole life.

We just have to focus on the big dream; targets put a plan and strategy in place and ride out the journey, so we can head to our destination

Think about waking up each and every morning knowing that all your hard work and the big dream has paid off , how would you feel right now.

You would be brimming with victory, bouncing around confidence and an extra spice of enthusiasm for your life, if you succeed, your attitude will change for the better which will lead to greater opportunities for both you and your family for life

The benefits of reaching a destination with a great outcome are exciting, I am the new me, and I like what I see, my life has change for good, if I can do it, you can achieve also. I know where I was

# How to become a conqueror of fear and negativity.

when I started to write the book, at the beginning of a journey, who ever thought I could write a book called the winners circle of dreams ,and I guess you are feeling the same way I did, whatever it is you wish to peruse, endure ,all things are so much possible if you want them badly enough,  Are you ready to take action and go for it, don't wait waste another minute of your time, set sail and cast off and go and pursue your dream, you are a winner

Here are 5 keynote tips to conquer fear and negativity

1 Flood your life positive thoughts and positive people
2 Become a warrior not a worrier
3 Seek out countless new opportunities.
4 Don't become the slave to fear and negativity.
5 You are the master of responsibility and take charge of your life.

Obstacles, Fear, Negativity, can't stop you. Problems can't stop you. Most of all other people can't stop you. Only you can stop you
**-Jeffrey Gitomer**

It may sound strange, but many champions are made champions by setbacks.
**-Bob Richards**


No matter how many times you fall down in your life it matters how you rise up and get back up again you are the winner.

## If I can do it, you can to, Imagine the possibilities.

I take my hat off to you because you have made a commitment to endure till the end to get through reading all the chapters in the book winners circle of dreams. One again if you have the dream to dream just do it ,as I have said to everybody if I can do it ,you can to ,you just have to believe it is something you want to do and you are prepared to do whatever it takes to stay in the dream long enough so you will win . Just imagine the time and the consistent effort commitment that you have put into your dream and the rewards that will be waiting just around the corner.

When you work on a goal or dream, and you have put in the hard yards completed and finished, you do feel relieved and looking back at your journey you feel so passionate and proud about what you have achieved

You may have tried or want to experience, running a marathon or doing a iron man event, you may have run 100km, when you look back at what you done, you put in the many nights of strength training and conditioning and running and swimming in, you were prepared for the starting line and endured physically and mentally the pain and heat to cross finish across the line.

This is what takes place in your life
Here are 10 keynote possibilities tips
1 You have achieved the Ultimate dream.
2 Time to celebrate and party
3 You see a transformation in the new you, what you have become.
4 Bask in Your own Success.
5 Excited and happy.
6 Inspired.

# If I can do it, you can to, Imagine the possibilities.

**7** Recognition,Benefits.
**8** Health is excellent.
**9** Open up to future opportunities.
**10** Winners' mentality, have the ability to achieve any other dreams and goals through out a life time.

"In order to <u>DREAM & SUCCEED,</u> your desire for success should be greater than your fear of failure." **- Bill Cosby.**

No matter how many times you fall down in your life it matters how you rise up and get back up again you are the winner.

# CHAPTER 9 NOTES

## Chapter 10

## 3Ds.3Rs.3Es.3As.3Ms Powerful DREAM Principles.

# *3 D.D.D

**Dream** Dream big, dream big, dream big, don't stop and you will win, we all have the power to the dream, our creator has given us the vision, as human beings, our thoughts are limitless Dream big, nothing is impossible but possible and very exciting.
Most people cannot see themselves dreaming the big dream, in fact, ever having a dream. They are fearful and scared to take a risk and chance anything in life .if you could just sit down and think about where your big dream can take you, if you made a commitment today to dream big and write them down , you will be see the future and end up a winner.

**Decide** Look Don't wait for others to decide what your top dream is, start giving yourself permission first to prepare for the start of your race, so sooner you front up at the start line you will feel good, have you ever had to make a quick decision on the spot, it's a similar feeling that comes into play or risk doing something unusual, or have you heard someone say I've got a gut feeling, that's called trust in your instincts. When you decide to do something, you are ready to make a change, which is great, and you have said I want to move on wards and up; you have given yourself the authority to plan and look forward to a brighter future

I have had different jobs all of my life and at 52 i didn't know I would be writing a book or doing motivational speaking, you see life is rather funny at times.

# 3Ds Powerful Dream Principles

**Determination**  How determined are you to not give up on your dreams and goals, are things in your life going to plan, determination is so important because it gives you that extra sense of hope that will help you across the finish line of life, just keep going and don't stop, always remember to look at your goals and dreams as I did, I look at mine on the fridge every day, and blogged inserts from winners circle of dreams to keep the dream alive.

Ants are amazing creatures they are great workers and team players, even the size of my feet which became the obstacle for them didn't deter them from getting their chores done, they were determined and just kept going over, under and around my feet

Doesn't matter how big the obstacles are for ants, I can assure you for their size and never say die character guts courage and determination, ants cease opportunity, they will just keep going and never give up, we to can adopt the ants determination to achieve our dreams and goals, we as human beings can stay focus to our task, solve problems and overcome, find a way to get around an obstacle. Ants they haven't got time for an obstacle to detract them from their busy working life and neither should we.

# 3Rs Powerful Dream Principles

## *3 R.R.R

**Reason** What is your reason? for wanting to do something different, or special, you must find that reason for change before anything can happen, I know 20 years ago a man and woman who had come to dinner changed our thoughts and lives forever, they gave us a reason for hope, made us dream of the possibilities through a big dream, goals, desire, and eagerness and action, they believed any ones dream could become a reality on the path to success. All you have to do is find out the reason, why, what, how, anything is achievable, John and Helen mentioned that night also how they dreamt that computers and a thing call network marketing and the world wide web were going to revolutionize how we buy our goods and service, also how we could keep our fulltime jobs and earn a living, work part-time and earn a fortune

Isn't funny how dreams become reality 20 YEARS ago that network company that john and Helen talked to my friends and I about called Amway has evolved into a worldwide global company and is still positioned as one of the strongest fortune 500 companies in America .

**Rough** Did you know most people see the end product of Diamonds that produces a magnificent shining light most amazingly .A rough diamond is a dull adaptable and unique piece of rock is buried in mud & darkness, beneath the earth's crust and surface and it still come out of its location, and still hasn't changed its true life form amazingly it can only reflects a shining light once it comes up from above the earth's surface.

It can happen with dreams and goals we can go through a rough patch in our lives we all tend to have our good days and bad days working on them , Weather storms are the same they swirl twirl and up lift everything in its path, when the storm has passed it is time to rebuild and start a fresh. How prepared are you to ride out the rough in your life,

# 3Rs Powerful Dream Principles

Maybe you are going through that rough patch right now whether it is your business and finance, relationship, then just maybe it's time to make a change to decide how things can actually be better

It's not what happens to you in rough times its time to take a stand to get tough and smart.

When we fall down in life it matters how we rise up and get back up again.

**Resolve** I say it is better to resolve, don't let your dream and goal be a hindrance and dissolve as you pursue to getting to where you are going , just remember the past doesn't have any bearing on the actions you take and your success in the future.

I was prepared to lay down those past skeletons in the closet and get excited about the future if I didn't I could not have written the book winners circle of dreams

Many people stay trapped in their past and are fearful of the future. You see when I get lost in my music it takes me back to the past both, good and some bad, what I am trying to say to you is we can tend to dwell in the how things use to be, and spend the whole time talking about how hard things can be instead, resolving an obstacle, to continue carving out happy life for our future. We can take a look at our past, learn from it and not get stuck in it

For some people, the past is like mind prison, you are under lock and key and there is no way out of the mind prison. You see, you believe you don't have freedom to do the things you want to do, and the obstacle called attitude, fear, failure, and the past strips you from achieving your big dreams and goals in life. It is your thoughts that put a restriction, negativity hurt and fear into your body mind and soul, one again your dreams and goals are waiting. For you to become a winner resolve your issues and obstacles today and don't dissolve in them.

A good friend of mine said to me we can deal with what life throws at us at times, to resolve is the best solution without resolve, we couldn't get a fantastic result.

# 3Es Powerful Dream Principles

## *3 E.E.E

**Excuses** Excuses, we all do it every day, the world we live in today is filled with so many distractions which lead to excuses, an excuse can be the key to our own demise, excuses are our nemesis and will stop us from achieving what we know. we are capable of. I need take responsibility for my excuses because I have been lazy and irresponsible and done little to show my progress for moving forward. in the life of real business and keeping your job these days there is no place for excuses, time is money and money is time if you were on face book in work time and you're not really focused on the company work, it can become an excuse, meaning face book take more president over your job. We need to take charge of those excuses which are holding us back, take action today and get mad scream or shout out, talk to yourself and say today is the day, enough is enough I deserve more in life and I aint going to let excuses be my obstacle, I want to be successful and excuses aint going to stop me from getting what I want. Conquer all your excuses take control today; show your excuses I am the master and not the slave

**Excited** People who dream get excited about the possibilities and believe that something great is going to happen today, and you are excited about making a change for you , have you ever felt this way , adventurous travel over sees to see different countries for the first time, jumping out of a plane ,do something crazy, and you seize the moment to chance your arm and take a risk to explore, I was at a major rugby final here in New Zealand and wow people get so excited about being amongst the hype and atmosphere of finals rugby , are your excited about a new idea, going on vacation, starting a new business , a new relationship , your first house, the new job promotion , getting new grades at your course , some of the many opportunist opportunities

your dreams work on the same principle as getting enthusiastic excited ,because you can see the long term benefits of an outcome that you have chosen, staying focused and excited keeps me locked

# 3Es Powerful Dream Principles

into my dream, we all have the power to get excited about something in our lives . When you know you are excited

about something, you are the winner, here is a remedy for having a happy and long lasting life, do that something you have always dreamed of, get excited about whatever it is today, and don't wait, the more you get excited about what it is you want in life, the closer you will get, to having what you want

**Endurance** Endure until the end, how can you win something for you if you don't see it through to the end, when was the last time you herd of a major sports team NFL ,baseball cricket ,soccer basketball ,rugby, Americas cup   quit half way through the season or the regatta , The great American migration from the East Coast over the icy rocky mountains of America did just that endured to open up the wild west of California the sunny state, many had a reason and a dream, endured, survived while others literally died, or quit. A lot of people didn't make it, not because they were bad, the ones that made it were fortunate, but they were the best because of what they endured. You see when you endure it meant never give up never quit, to the end, and simply be the last ones standing, great dreams great companies  and great relationship and marriage have one thing in common, endurance till the end and have reap the rewards

Sometimes we don't know when our breakthrough in life will come. So don't guarantee your failure by quitting or buy your current condition. You can adapt, change, and evolve, and modify, but never, never, never quit.

Always believe in the power of the Big Dream and the unlimited potential you have

When your life seems overcast, foggy, rocky, stormy, they do, and will decline, it's time to grab your time in the sun again. And there will be many times in one's life, you think there is no such thing as hope ,and you are defeated, but don't forget to count the many blessings and victories you've won.

# 3As Powerful Dream Principles

## *3 A.A.A.

**Ambitious** Are you eager and ambitious about your dreams and goals they must be ardently desired to change and be disciplined

Bite your finger nails if you have too, if you want that dream and goal to happen, you will find a way of making it happen you have to have that ambition and desire locked in your heart because if you are really so serious you will not give up at all, no matter the costs because you want those things so bad.

Most people mite "just like small things" they won't pay the price for it, because "just like small things" are easy to acquire, and you don't have to pay a hefty price to go out and get them,

Do you know the saddest people in life, is a person who is always says they going to get started on something, and they are busy doing nothing

I Close my eyes and think of the person I was 5 yrs. ago what I had , what I was doing , "I had nothing and broke" I don't want to go back to doing the same thing as I did 5 years ago ,im hoping to in next 5 – 20 will be even more ambitious and brighter for my family and It would be , the sad truth in life is in five years from today if you don't have an ambitious dream and goal or even attempt to try something new in your life that you desire You will be in the same situation you are in now, If you don't decide what you want for you , who knows you how bright your future will be

I can't make you do anything, all I can do is try my best to inspire, encourage you, what you want to do, and to figure out how to get it.

**Attitude** is one of the most powerful key principles of winning , to becoming successful "Attitude is everything" it can be the difference between winning and losing ,dreaming about the future, wanting to change or just trying something new in your life and is all about having a great attitude , making a choice and dealing with people from all walks of life, is all about having a great attitude , think about this who is your centre of influence , who are the

# 3As Powerful Dream Principles

people that stand out from the crowd , why do we follow people who are successful in their own right , they have a positive outlook always smiling and reaching for the stars in their life. When we get excited and do well, our attitude changes, and goes to another level.

Words and what we say, have a powerful influence toward our attitude, when we say something bad or negative our whole body language sinks to a lower level , it could make or break our thinking patterns ,influence and have bearing on the start of a new day.

Negative attitudes won't get you anywhere in life, just ask people who have negative and bitter attitudes, have friends, they usually lead, unhappy, in a rut and lonely lives.

Everybody has the right to choose the attitude they want and desire, they just have, 2 to pick from, a positive outlook or a negative outlook on life.

What is it that we all do when spring is in the air, our attitude changes there a spring in our personality, have you ever watched the monarch butterfly so busy flying around seemingly ever so graceful, with a countless amazing attitude, they're such beautiful creatures With such a short life cycle the monarch attitude is to focus on staying busy to focus on the tasks in hand from laying eggs to a little caterpillar to a cocoon and then emerges as a butterfly the monarch butterfly once more.

Top of the list predators for the butterfly is the spider, have you seen the ways the spider takes full advantage and control ,the victims chance of breaking free from the web are pretty remote.

The spider attitude is to railroad in fact, kidnap their victims first, paralyze, and poison them full bitterness

With humans it can be the same, we can take up monarch butterfly attitude or take on the spider's attitude and make a misery of people's lives and big dreams inject them with the poison of bitterness.

# 3As Powerful Dream Principles

**Action**, for anyone to be successful at anything in life, you have to take evasive action .Taking action is the heart and soul and ticket to success performance and outcome. There is no other way out, if you don't take action, do nothing and get nothing, or you can take action to take that risk, you will try something for that greater chance of winning for you.

I have to action my time to generate a productive way to go forward in my life and achieve winning results, you see so many people say they would like to achieve something great in their lives, they know what the outcome and possibilities are,

Big dreamers and top achievers action what it is they want to achieve , they start at the start line and begin to take small , medium , and giant steps to move forward at all times. The day I see a marathon runner and basketball player win a race or win a game from the side line will be amazing If you action your dreams and goals from the start, you will produce productivity to create the outcome you so call desire, Successful people in life already have actioned and planned what the next sets of strategies are, and have another goal immediately in mind.

## 3Ms Powerful Dream Principles

## *3 M.M.M.

**Motivation** How motivated are you, to go out and achieve your most important dreams and goals today , if you have read this and are just about to give up ,I have news for you stayed focused and relaxed and don't contemplate on quitting

We all have big dreams and aspirations, what are we going to do about it to take the dream to the next level, no matter how big the dream or little the chore, we know we have to take ownership and responsibility to get things done, motivation happens once you have a clear road map of destination and action a set task and focus 100% on what it is I need to get me there.

## "Commit to a time frame to stay motivated"

 If you're that person that likes to plan ahead, mark your dreams and goals, with a corresponding time frame, on your calendar. Doing this a week or so in advance will help you get motivated as you will be setting a goal that you can look forward to accomplishing. Remember a champion will work on getting the task done today and not leave it for tomorrow, because they are happy to see the task done   say to yourself that you are going to start working on the task done,  now and give it a clear finished time and date, whether it's finished or not. Motivation helps us in so many ways and gives us a real sense of value, it is worth it once you complete those task and they are pencilled off the to-do list and should be enough to keep you motivated and keep you that way. Isn't it nice when you know your are making headway and going forward Strive to be a Motivation conqueror motivate and conquer what it's you have to do

A good friend of mine said to me you must put the quality time in to take your business to another level, during your set time, eliminate all possible distractions that could turn into

# 3Ms Powerful Dream Principles

procrastination switch off the cell phone radio, and disable your internet. Tell your friends that you need time out to complete a

Specific job.

Once your time frame has ended, just take some time out,


Reward yourself, if you have completed a task, If I can get the next task done today, say I will go to a movie with my wife or go out to Wendy's
Reward is great for positive satisfaction so chill out and have some fun on the way to your journey and destination of success

In order to stay motivated, focus on small, actions and gains made You will be amazed at how much of those little things get done real quickly and learn, adapt and find faster more efficient ways to really make some dents in what you are trying to accomplish

**Momentum**
Personal dreams and goals need momentum, it's one of the key principles that will determine how far you have gone in life, also how quickly you would like to get to your destination. Momentum is a key driving force to everything you wish to pursue in life.

One way to gain momentum is to see where our target is, write down your dreams and goals with purpose and action

We all have a dream and goal in mind — I have given you some key tips about how to change , maybe you know already or have got something better in mind, and that's ok .but don't let your mind pursued you, to not give what ever it is a go, what we tend to do ,is not write our dreams or goals down, we cant see them on paper on the fridge or in a journal so we go blind lose our momentum and can not measure how we are going with our performances .
Whether it is making an appointment, with your bank manager, racing in the 100 metre sprint champs , having a baby, running a marathon, climbing the highest mountains, losing weight, putting on new make up, buying a pet, saving up for that new car or that first house or trip around the world, or alternatively wanting to

# 3Ms Powerful Dream Principles

change jobs for some career ambition, have them written down on paper somewhere so you can see ,where we have to go cross the finish line, If you don't see any momentum going forward in your life, then you can quickly become dishearten.

Establishing a plan with action, a target with a time line will help you work towards gaining momentum changing and achieving and getting all the things you want in life, you will get motivated and keep focused stay on track, it also helps prevent you from just drifting along and falling into a rut — so remember with every dream or goal you wish to pursue along with momentum and drive

The quicker you use your momentum to get to your destination that is the difference between the winners and the losers in life?

**Measure** For your dreams and goals to become reality they must be measured each step of the way, most sport people and major companies measure their success based on results called key performance indicators and measure performance and results at business, work place and on the sports field.

An outcome and result is the best indicators for process and depict, where we at are. Are you on the right track to hitting your dream, goal or target and achieving the outcome?

Always take a measure of ones progress, you could mistake action and process for productivity, meaning people say they are busy, but busy making no headway at all and have lost productivity.

# The Finale Summary © 2012

Wow I did it; "you have read the stories in my book" and have followed me on my journey "what now for you"? What is it you, would like to achieve in your in life"? Remember its up is to you.

All you need is to take that giant leap of faith with action.
With the <u>time</u> you have available on this earth, "really" what is it you would like to have, to be the best at what you would like to become.

Are you comfortable with the life you have now, that's ok?
If we are to ever take ourselves to a new and higher level in our life, we must be willing to get out of the square box of our comfort zone too challenge to find our true potential "believe me" when I say, there is no other way.

Like any dream or goal, working on my first book winner's circle of dreams heading towards the outcome, was never going be easy.

The Challenges and obstacles, we face each and every day of our lives are there for a purpose, they teach us to be stronger and help to make a change from ordinary to be extraordinary.

I always knew if I stayed focused and disciplined, endured the dream of becoming an Author and Speaker, it would turn into reality and also make big impact so gratifying, I faced the obstacles head on and overcome I won, opportunities are about to open up a whole new world I could never have dreamed were possible, to measure one self, and how far I have become, and grown as a person ,and the value I have given others ,as a result of who and what they have become, it's so unbelievable.

We can all talk the talk hear about success but are you ready to action the talk.

No matter how many times you fall down in your life it matters how you rise up and get back up again you are the winner

Keep reaching for the stars.

www.ingramcontent.com/pod-product-compliance
Lightning Source LLC
Chambersburg PA
CBHW071455040426
42444CB00008B/1342